D1202038

Cities and Immigrants

A GEOGRAPHY OF CHANGE IN
NINETEENTH-CENTURY AMERICA

A GEOGRAPHY OF CHANGE IN

NINETEENTH-CENTURY AMERICA

Cities and Immigrants

DAVID WARD

NEW YORK
OXFORD UNIVERSITY PRESS
LONDON 1971 TORONTO

TO JUDY

301.36
W 25c

Copyright © 1971 by Oxford University Press, Inc.
Library of Congress Catalogue Card Number: 74-124612
Printed in the United States of America

FOREWORD

Cities and Immigrants is one of two books by which Oxford University Press is inaugurating a series of succinct but, we trust, stimulating volumes in a little cultivated field of American historical scholarship—that which is usually called historical geography or geographical history. We prefer to think of them as studies of changing geography or of geographical change. Those of us engaged in the enterprise are, for the most part, professional geographers, and, although historians will form a substantial sector of our readership and we address ourselves to them as much as to geographers or other social scientists, our central and vital concern with place, location, and interaction or diffusion through space clearly identifies us in our own profession.

The other completed volume is Donald Meinig's *Southwest: Three Peoples in Geographical Change,* which interprets the evolution of the cultural geography of a quadrant of the United States diametrically opposite to the one where Ward's major interest is concentrated. Other studies soon to join these include a double volume on the historical geography of Canada, and separate treatments of colonial New England and the colonial southern seaboard. These we expect to be followed by studies of the middle colonies, the first Trans-Appalachian expansion, the ante-bellum Midwest and the Gulf South, and a new interpretation of the Great Plains, and special studies of California and the Pacific Northwest. Our ultimate hope is to supply a small library of thematic studies of different places and times in our continental development that can serve as joint or supplemental texts for college and university

AUG 13 '71

HUNT LIBRARY
CARNEGIE-MELLON UNIVERSITY

courses in history and geography. We will miss our mark, however, if each volume does not provide something of a new interpretative adventure.

David Ward was educated at the University of Leeds and it was there that both his professional interest in cities and his career of post-graduate study began. This he completed with a doctorate at the University of Wisconsin. He then taught for some years in Canada before returning to Madison where he is now an associate professor. His Wisconsin dissertation was focused upon Boston and its changing internal geography during the period of most active immigration to that city in the nineteenth and early twentieth centuries. Since then he has directed his attention to a variety of American cities. One of the more important factors in the changing nature of American cities and in the major characteristics of their growth was the vast inflow of immigrants from the 1820's to the 1920's, and Ward's concern with the initiation and changing character of ethnic ghettoes is clearly reflected in this volume.

Although studies based upon quantitative data (especially of the manuscript census returns to the degree that they are now available), have been drawn upon as broadly as possible in this volume, much fundamental quantitative analysis remains to be done. An attempt has, however, been made to review a wide variety of generalizations or models of urban characteristics and growth, including those that have been advanced by economic historians and ecologically-minded sociologists. Neither in the development or testing of theory, nor in the development of new hypotheses from empirical work, has much attention been paid in the past to changing locational or spatial considerations. It is to such matters, in terms of what we would call the geography of urban change, or changing urban geography, that this volume is devoted. Its purpose is to help us make a little more sense of the industrial/urban development of the United States in the nineteenth and early twentieth centuries.

ANDREW H. CLARK

Madison, Wisconsin
February 1970

PREFACE

This small volume is the outgrowth of my efforts to teach a course which is partly concerned with the changing urban geography of the United States during the nineteenth century. The bibliographic materials available for such a course are voluminous in several disciplines and this book has attempted to digest only those contributions which either implicitly or explicitly have examined the spatial dimensions of urbanization. My own research has been heavily focused upon the internal spatial structure of residential areas in northeastern American cities during the nineteenth century but I have attempted to venture into less familiar ground and discuss aspects of the external relations of cities. Naturally my debts are numerous, especially to students who reacted to verbal or preliminary versions of these chapters and Ted Muller in particular provided many useful comments. My colleague and general editor of this series, Andrew Clark offered many stimulating suggestions as did another colleague, Bill Clark. I am of course responsible for the limitations of the final result.

DAVID WARD

Madison, Wisconsin
March 1970

CONTENTS

FIGURES

PHOTOGRAPHS

TABLES

Cities and Immigrants

A GEOGRAPHY OF CHANGE IN

NINETEENTH-CENTURY AMERICA

INTRODUCTION

During the period of mass immigration between about 1820 and 1920, urban growth in the United States attained new and unparalleled dimensions. By far the largest number of immigrants settled in urban centers and thereby compounded the local concentration of an already rapidly growing resident population. This book considers some of the geographical aspects and implications of urbanization in the United States during that century of fast growth.

Contemporary urbanization in the Western World derives its magnitude and complexity from spectacular increases in population growth and redistribution during the past one hundred and fifty years. These changes happened to parallel the Industrial Revolution, but it should be noted that, while urbanization and industrialization are closely related, they are nevertheless generically distinct processes. Historically there are examples of urban growth without industrial development and of productive innovations in distinctly rural settings,[1] and even today rapid urbanization is taking place in many parts of the underdeveloped world, accompanied by little advance in per capita productivity. But in the economically advanced world, despite considerable differences in timing, the acceleration in urbanization and increases in productivity occurred almost simultaneously. There were also concurrent changes in social organization, institutions, political life, individual and group behavior, and cultural characteristics.[2] Partly for these reasons the interpretive implications and chronological limits of the term "Industrial Revolution" have become matters of historiographic controversy. Definitions of urbanization have also aroused a considerable debate, but recent discussions have tended to emphasize the rate and dimensions of the process of population concentration itself, rather than its structural characteristics, which too frequently lack universality.[3]

Any increase in the rate of urbanization or population concentration tends to encourage the selective growth and internal differentiation of urban centers. Thus, changes are produced not only in their locational patterns and hierarchical ordering but also in the internal arrangement of their populations and functions. The changing spatial characteristics of urban centers have been related to the new locational possibilities created by advances in technology and organization. For example, "industrial" and "metropolitan" phases in regional economic organization have been distinguished on the basis of differences in selective urban growth.[4] During the industrial phase, changes in technology stimulated the concentration of production and the enlargement of market areas, thereby supporting the growth of certain market towns which had previously served the needs of local exchange only. Some of these centers eventually assumed preeminent positions in the intra-regional economy and in inter-regional trade. As metropolitan cities emerged, their hinterlands were partitioned into market areas served by a related hierarchy of service centers. Presumably, most of the settlements which had expanded during the "industrial" phase without the support of metropolitan functions assumed an appropriate place in the urban hierarchy during this "metropolitan" stage.

An alternative suggestion is that metropolitan centers existed long before lower-order centers;[5] that, in the initial stages of urbanization, a few large cities provided the urban needs of vast areas. Lower-order settlements grew subsequently by industrializing or by providing services for the surrounding areas. The implication is that metropolitan centers dominated the external relations of the regional economy long before the productive potential of any particular area had been realized. In contrast, the former interpretation argues that many settlements had harnessed local resources before metropolitan centers began to concentrate inter-regional trade. In spite of their differences, both schemes hypothesize similar terminal phases. Indeed, during the first two decades of the present century, radical changes in transportation and communication slowed down the subdivision of metropolitan hinterlands and the multiplication of service centers. Higher-order settlements began to capture market areas once controlled by lower-order settlements, while activities and services tended to reconcentrate in but a few high-order centers.[6]

Spatial changes in urban growth were paralleled by alterations in the arrangements of people and activities within cities as well. For example, in pre-industrial cities, the most affluent and prestigious residents occupied central locations. The poorest people lived on the edges of the city; the artisans and the tradesmen between the rich and the poor. This arrangement of socio-economic groups has been attributed to the prestige attached to central locations by pre-industrial societies and the ability of the well-to-do to obtain dwellings within walking distance of administrative and commercial facilities.[7] With the expansion of commerce and industry in the city center, the value of maximum accessibility to urban facilities was increasingly offset by a deterioration of the residential environment. Thus, peripheral locations isolated from undesirable adjacent land uses (but within reasonable reach of central business areas) became attractive to high-income residents. The dwellings they vacated, once subdivided and extended with cheap new structures, provided a new and centrally located supply of low-rent housing. If the supply of central residences was inadequate to meet the needs of a rapidly growing population, then peripheral shanty towns continued to house low-income immigrants. However, with the introduction of new and cheap forms of local transportation, middle-income people joined the suburban movement and most low-income and immigrant families concentrated in old housing near the expanding centrally located employment opportunities.

During the second half of the nineteenth century streetcars, horse-drawn at first and later electrically powered, increased the potential length of the journey to work, making possible the dispersal of a growing proportion of the urban population. Since the new streetcar suburbs were limited to those able to afford more spacious housing and the time and cost of a longer journey to work, very few newly-arrived immigrants and low-income people were able to leave their congested central quarters, and absolute population declines in the central immigrant quarters of many cities did not occur until after World War I. Quite apart from the failure of the expanding streetcar systems to arrest immigrant congestion in central residential districts, local commodity movements within cities remained extremely expensive until the introduction of the motor truck. For this reason, the decentralization of employment pro-

TABLE 0-1

Growth of the Urban Population of the United States, 1790–1920

	Total Population (by 1000's)	Urban Population (by 1000's)	Per Cent Urban	Per Cent Growth of Urban Population	Per Cent Growth of Total Population
1790	3,929	201	5.1		
1800	5,308	322	6.1	60	35
1810	7,239	525	7.3	69	36
1820	9,638	693	7.2	33	33
1830	12,866	1,127	8.8	82	34
1840	17,069	1,845	10.8	68	33
1850	23,191	3,543	15.3	99	36
1860	31,443	6,216	19.8	75	36
1870	39,818	9,902	25.7	59	23
1880	50,155	14,129	28.2	40	30
1890	62,947	22,106	35.1	61	25
1900	75,994	30,159	39.7	36	21
1910	91,972	41,998	45.7	39	21
1920	105,710	54,157	51.2	29	15

vided little additional incentive to suburban residence until after the turn of the century.

Compact and congested forms of nineteenth-century urban growth frequently have been distinguished from the more open and diffuse forms of growth that characterize the present century. Sir Patrick Geddes, the pioneer human ecologist, attributed these differences to the passing of a "paleo-technic era" in which steam power was the main source of energy, and the advent of a "neo-technic era" in which electricity and petroleum became increasingly important.[8] During the "paleo-technic era," most but not all employment was concentrated in and adjacent to central urban locations, and the labor force was concentrated within walking distance of these areas. During the "neo-technic era," some types of employment were gradually decentralized and some segments of the labor force were able to live at considerable distances from their jobs. In spite of these new locational possibilities of the "neo-technic" era, many of the urban processes and patterns established and supported during the "paleo-technic" era endured at least into the second and third decades of the present century. For these reasons, the longevity of the urban features associated with the "paleo-technic" era remain a matter of debate but their highly localized beginnings occurred in areas which also displayed a marked acceleration in their rates of urbanization.

In the United States the rate of urbanization increased quite markedly after about 1840 for, although the urban proportion of the population had doubled since 1800, in the two decades before the Civil War, this proportion almost doubled again to 20 per cent (Table 0-1). Indeed, between 1800 and 1840 the rates of urbanization fluctuated (even decelerating between 1810 and 1820 and again between 1830 and 1840), and it was in the forties that the largest decennial rate increase was recorded. This acceleration was partly supported by the beginnings of large-scale foreign immigration. New England and the Middle Atlantic states had the largest proportion of the urban population and attracted most of the new immigrants, but increasing numbers were moving to the cities in the West (Table 0-2).

Between 1860 and 1900, the urban proportion of the population doubled once more to 40 per cent and by 1920 exceeded one-half of the total population. After modest declines between 1850 and 1880, the decennial rate of growth increased again between 1880 and 1890. By 1900 the continental pattern of metropolitan centers was firmly established, and the major industrial cities of the northeastern manufacturing belt had become the most populous urban centers in the nation. Moreover,

TABLE 0-2

Urban Population of the United States by Census Regions, 1790–1920

	Percentage of Total Population Urban				
	United States	Northeast	North Central	South	West
1790	5.1	8.1		2.1	
1800	6.1	9.3		3.0	
1810	7.3	10.9	0.9	4.1	
1820	7.2	11.0	1.1	4.6	
1830	8.8	14.2	2.6	5.3	
1840	10.8	18.5	3.9	6.7	
1850	15.3	26.5	9.2	8.3	6.4
1860	19.8	35.7	13.9	9.6	16.0
1870	25.7	44.3	20.8	12.2	25.8
1880	28.2	50.8	24.2	12.2	30.2
1890	35.1	59.0	33.1	16.3	37.0
1900	39.7	61.1	38.6	18.0	39.9
1910	45.7	71.8	45.1	22.5	47.9
1920	51.2	75.5	52.3	28.1	51.8

Note: for boundaries see fig. 1-2.

toward the end of the nineteenth century striking regional variations in the rates and extent of urbanization finally started to diminish.

The spread of urbanization was accompanied by a rearrangement and expansion of population and activities within cities. By 1900 the central business districts of older cities alone occupied an area equivalent to the entire urban settlement at the beginning of the century. The physical enlargement of the American city was quite limited by present-day standards, yet the separation of home and work and the suburban movement had been established, and the most characteristic aspects of modern cities and the modern urban systems had emerged. Other equally dominant and areally more extensive dimensions of modern urban life are of more recent origin and owe their spatial characteristics to new flexibility in transportation and communication and an increase in mass purchasing power. Although the outward movement of the urban population and the decline of the small town was well publicized before 1920, it was only after that date that the spatial characteristics of urban settlements established during the nineteenth century were radically altered. (In the chapters that follow, the spatial effects of selective urban growth and internal differentiation are investigated. The effects of regional economic growth and migration upon urbanization are the topics of the first two chapters; the remaining three consider the internal differentiation of urban settlements. Social scientists of several disciplines have studied the spatial characteristics of urban settlements, and many of their generalizations provide retrospective and generally deductive insights into the growth of the modern cities. In recognition of this, each chapter first offers generalizations on the course of change, or proposes developmental models before describing specific changes in the extent and form of urban growth. The most widely accepted interpretations of nineteenth century urbanization emphasize those consistent elements of change which bequeath enduring arrangements to the present. Yet, these discussions also recognize ephemeral elements as well as regional and national variations in the developmental process.)

In some but not all of the following chapters, the generalizations are derived in part from the small but growing body of historical scholarship which is based upon quantitative data and statistical analysis. These quantitative studies have attempted to establish general developmental trends in the growth and composition of urban populations, or alternatively to test and elaborate existing historiographic contentions based primarily upon qualitative evidence. Moreover, the theoretical postulates of the contemporary social sciences have also been utilized as a source of new hypotheses appropriate to quantitative historical studies.[9] For several decades, cross-fertilization in economic theory and economic history has indirectly contributed to our understanding of the development of the national or regional systems of cities and these inter-disciplinary works now complement the narrative and interpretative accounts of the commercial fortunes and rivalries of individual and usually populous cities.[10] But at this time, the spatial characteristics of an evolving regional system of cities, in particular the growth behavior of small urban centers, remains obscure. Similarly, there have been few empirical investigations of cityward movement in the United States, although in a study of Swedish towns, Morrill has provided a pioneering examination of the changing relationship between migration and urbanization.[11]

Quantitative studies of the internal characteristics of cities have concentrated on social mobility and on the characteristics or behavior of particular groups within the city.[12] But the ecological implications of these studies have rarely been explored, and our knowledge of the changing location and structure or urban employment nodes are largely dependent on narrative accounts of changes in land use in a few centers. Consequently, the evidence and methodology of works discussed in this book are quite varied. Most of the generalizations in Chapter 1 (Urbanization and Regional Economic Development) and Chapter 5 (Local Transportation and Suburban Expansion) are based upon a variety of narrative descriptions and quantitative examinations, but interpretative statements in the other chapters are in general based upon sources with a more limited empirical and conceptual coverage.)

NOTES

1. T. O. Wilkinson, "Urban Structure and Industrialization," *American Sociological Review*, 25, 1960, pp. 353-63; B. F. Hozelitz, "The City, The Factory and Economic Growth," *American Economic Review*, 45, 1955, pp. 166-84; E. E. Lampard, "The History of Cities in the Economically Advanced Areas," *Economic Development and Cultural Change*, 3, 1955, pp. 81-136.
2. W. E. Moore, *The Impact of Industry*, Englewood Cliffs, N.J., 1965, pp. 85-111; N. J. Smelser, *Social Change in the Industrial Revolution—An Application of Theory to the British Cotton Industry: 1770-1840*, Chicago, 1959, pp. 384-408;

R. E. Turner, "The Industrial City: Center of Cultural Change," in C. F. Ware, ed., *The Cultural Approach to History*, New York, 1940, pp. 228-42.

3. E. E. Lampard, 'Historical Aspects of Urbanization," in P. M. Hauser and L. F. Schnore, eds., *The Study of Urbanization*, New York, 1965, pp. 519-54.

4. N. S. B. Gras, *An Introduction to Economic History*, New York, 1922.

5. W. R. Thompson, *A Preface to Urban Economics*, Baltimore, 1965, pp. 15-16.

6. B. J. L. Berry, *Geography of Market Centers and Retail Distribution*, Englewood Cliffs, N.J., 1967, pp. 5-9; J. E. Brush and H. L. Gauthier, Jr., "Service Centers and Consumer Trips: Studies on the Philadelphia Metropolitan Fringe," *Department of Geography Research Paper No. 113*, Chicago, 1968, p. 30.

7. G. Sjoberg, *The Pre-industrial City*, New York, 1960, pp. 91-105; L. F. Schnore, "On the Spatial Structure of Cities in the Two Americas," in P. F. Hauser and L. F. Schnore, eds., *The Study of Urbanization*, New York, 1965, pp. 347-98; J. E. Vance, Jr., "Labor-shed, Employment Field, and Dynamic Analysis in Urban Geography," *Economic Geography*, 36, 1960, pp. 189-220.

8. P. E. Geddes, *Cities in Evolution*, London, rev. ed., 1949, pp. 60-108.

9. W. O. Aydelotte, "Quantification in History," *American Historical Review*, 71, 1966, pp. 803-25; A. R. Pred, *The Spatial Dynamics of U.S. Urban-Industrial Growth, 1800-1914: Interpretative and Theoretical Essays*, Cambridge, 1966; S. Thernstrom and R. Sennett, "Preface" in S. Thernstrom and R. Sennett, eds., *Nineteenth-Century Cities: Essays in the New Urban History*, New Haven, 1969, pp. vii-xi and S. P. Hays, "The Use of Archives for Historical Statistical Inquiry," *Journal of the National Archives*, 1, 1969, pp. 7-15.

10. E. E. Lampard, "American Historians and the Study of Urbanization," *American Historical Review*, 67, 1961, pp. 49-61.

11. R. L. Morrill, "Migration and the Spread and Growth of Urban Settlement," *Lund Studies in Geography*, Series B, 26, 1965.

12. S. Thernstrom and R. Sennett, eds., *op. cit.*, pp. 1-244.

1 URBANIZATION AND

REGIONAL ECONOMIC DEVELOPMENT

Studies relating urbanization to economic growth identify the level of economic organization necessary to support urban life and show how changes in technology and productivity affect the degree of urbanization.[1] In most long-settled European countries, urban growth merely accompanied a gradual expansion of a market economy, whereas in the United States a dynamic market economy stimulated urbanization at the time of initial settlement. Several early theories of settlement, however, postulate a pre-urban phase when frontier areas were largely sustained by subsistence activities. Turner's "frontier" thesis, for example, implies that cities appeared long after the initial settlement of an area.[2] Presumably, the sequence of pioneering from fur trading to farming supported dispersed rural populations, and urban centers were created by subsequent concentrations of these frontiersmen. Gras proposes a somewhat similar sequence of urbanization but for both long and newly settled areas. His scheme offers a more explicit definition of changes in the process of selective growth by noting that financial functions in particular allowed a few settlements to dominate other towns within their hinterlands.[3]

An alternative "metropolitan" thesis questions an initial phase of subsistence pioneering and suggests that export and supply towns established soon after initial settlement provided even the most remote of North American settlements with rudimentary linkages to external markets.[4] There were, in fact, few such centers in the frontier areas, but there is considerable evidence that towns near the outer limits of new settlement not only supplied the pioneers with essential equipment but also provided marketing facilities for staples produced in the adjacent areas.[5] Certainly Douglass North's model of economic growth in the United States before 1860 implies the early development of commercial centers in the Old Northwest, not only for exports to the Northeast and to Europe, but also for trade with other newly-settled sections of North America.[6] Presumably, entrepôts were well established long before most smaller settlements had developed urban functions.

In contrast, Smolensky and Ratejczak argue that the division of labor and the advantages of occupational specialization stimulated local city growth for some time before inter-regional communications supported the growth of metropolitan centers.[7] Their conclusions are based on the dominance of locally oriented occupations in one western city before the arrival of the railroad. Rubin also suggests that the constant stream of new settlers into areas beyond the inland extension of railroads and canals provided "hidden" import mechanisms and local markets for surplus production.[8] The degree to which settlers stimulated urbanization and influenced the spatial pattern and density of urban centers has not been explored logically, and the proportionate impact of local service and export functions on the initial growth of frontier towns remains unclear. Certainly, the dimensions of those frontier cities which quickly established their regional primacy would have been more modest if some external markets had not been developed soon after initial settlement.

Once the initial settlement of an area was completed, however, local commercial developments strongly influenced urban growth. In particular, changes in employment or per capita productivity of the different sectors of the economy indicated an absolute and relative expansion for both services and goods.[9] Under these circumstances, local patterns of consumption rather than a distant demand for staple goods determined the rate and form of urbanization. Thompson has recently defined five stages of urban growth based on local commercial development.[10] The first three stages describe the transition from an economy dependent almost exclusively on the export of a single staple to one designed to serve diversified local needs. The two final stages represent alternative courses for further development and describe the process of metropolitan dominance in regional services or the establishment of national or international primacy in specialized goods or services. Occasionally individual cities will exhibit the characteristics of both final stages.

SELECTIVITY OF URBAN GROWTH

These discussions have been concerned primarily with the factors involved in city growth rather than with the regional and locational implications of differences in the rate and degree of urbanization in general. After considering the growth factors of a given city, Thompson concluded that rapid growth within the hierarchy of cities was usually based upon an early lead amply fortified with local leadership,[11] and Pred suggested that the largest cities were most likely long established ones—those having the advantage of an "early lead."[12] Pred specified these initial advantages of established centers as their local labor supply and their monopoly of many local services and of external market connections and financial facilities. These initial advantages stimulated the continued concentration of new activities, and the enlarged pool of capital and ingenuity created a receptive environment for further growth.

Although most metropolitan centers had initial advantages during their early periods of growth, many did not expand as anticipated. To explain this variation, Pred argues that accessibility to national markets, differences in railroad developments and the application of innovations had a marked effect on the ability of a given center to use its advantages fully. More recently Borchert concluded that major technological changes created new patterns of initial advantage, exemplified by three "epochs" during which urbanization was affected by similar types of movement and production.[13] Specifically, the period from 1830 to 1870 is characterized by the "Steamboat and Iron Horse," that from 1870 to 1920 by "Steel Rails and Electric Power," and that from 1920 to the present by the "Internal Combustion Engine and the Shift to Services." Although many large centers were able to exploit the possibilities of each new "epoch," others with more specialized commitments to an early technology faced partial eclipse or expensive adjustments. In short, technological changes either compounded or interrupted urban growth generated by initial advantages. Yet the eclipse of established cities was far from total, for although some failed to develop new activities, their old functions often endured to sustain a modest growth.[14]

Studies by Madden and Lukermann have helped to determine the relationship between aggregate results of urbanization and the growth of individual cities. Madden observes that the rank size distribution of

HUNT LIBRARY
CARNEGIE-MELLON UNIVERSITY

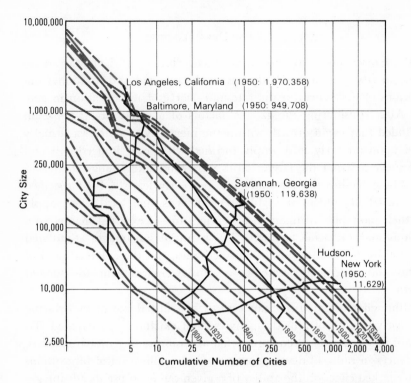

Source: C. H. Madden, "On Some Indicators of Stability
in the Growth of Cities in the United States," *Economic
Development and Cultural Change*, 4, 1956, p. 239.

FIG. 1-1. Rank-Size Distribution of American Cities, 1790-1950

American cities indicated an unusual degree of stability between 1790
and 1950, and although cities frequently changed rank between censuses,
the aggregate relationship between rank and the proportion of the total
population in each settlement did not change.[15] (Fig. 1-1). Lukermann's
study, which examined the rank size distribution of the first 100 rank-
ing settlements for the census years from 1790 to 1890 revealed a similar
stability, but he notes a trend toward greater growth in the largest cities
between 1810 and 1880.[16] This trend was most evident in 1860, when 80
per cent of the population of the ranked cities lived in the 30 largest
cities.

Lukermann also grouped the growth patterns for the leading 25 cities
(Fig. 1-2) and found that rank stability throughout the 100-year period
was limited to the major seaports that had dominated the urban life of

the nation from its inception. Several other settlements which were well established in 1790 declined in rank but maintained their place among the leading cities of 1890. Most of the smaller coastal and inland towns, however, were grouped as "dropouts" from the list of leading cities. A category of "rising" towns described interior settlements which gradually increased their rank, but the populations of most of the inland metropolises and industrial centers of 1890 increased so rapidly that within the span of one or two decades they were classified as "entries" into the list of leading ranked cities.[17] This type of grouping—even for a small number of cities—clearly illustrates the need to evaluate how the advantages of established and new locations affect urban growth. According to Lukermann, any adequate explanation of the settlement pattern awaits a careful reconstruction of the changing volume, direction, and complexity of the movements of people, goods, and information, which he calls the "circulation manifold."

Certainly such an investigation will include evaluations of the growth behavior of numerous lower-order centers. Regional studies, however, are faced with inadequate data for small centers and difficulties in defining the areal extent of metropolitan hinterlands. In a pioneer study of selective growth in the Northeast between 1820 and 1870, Williamson and Swanson found that initial advantage had no apparent influence on variations in growth.[18] Their primary concern, however, was with dynamics and not location, although they did attempt to link the growth characteristics of cities and hinterlands. More recently Higgs concluded that, in four Middle Western States between 1870 and 1900, the main source of city growth was the growth of the population of the surrounding countryside and certainly the growth of these Middle Western cities was not at the expense of their hinterland populations.[19]

Currently, the most satisfactory descriptions of spatial arrangements of settlements are based on Christaller's Central Place Theory, which argues that settlements of similar sizes and functions are equally spaced; consequently, their market areas form a hierarchy of hexagons which, theoretically at least, provides for maximum accessibility to local consumers.[20] Berry has applied this reasoning to the emergence of the urban hierarchy of southwestern Iowa.[21] There service centers frequently grew up around grist mills, railroad stations, courthouses or post offices, but subsequent growth depended on accessibility to local consumers. Moreover, as means of local movement and the needs of the local consumers changed, the distribution of service centers changed accordingly. Thus,

Classification

● Rank Stability
▲ Rising Rank
▼ Declining Rank
■ Rank Entry
□ Dropouts

The number following a city name
indicates its rank in size in 1890

FIG. 1-2. Growth Characteristics of Large American Cities, 1790-1890

CENTRAL

NORTH EAST

MINNEAPOLIS–ST. PAUL 8

MILWAUKEE 16

ROCHESTER 19

Schenectady

Portsmouth   Newburyport
Gloucester
Salem

BUFFALO 11

ALBANY 24   BOSTON 6
PROVIDENCE 21   New Bedford
Newport

DETROIT 15

NEW YORK 1

NEW LONDON
New London
HAVEN 28

CHICAGO 2

CLEVELAND 10

PITTSBURGH 13

Lancaster

PHILADELPHIA 3

MAHA 18

INDIANAPOLIS 23

CINCINNATI 9

BALTIMORE

KANSAS CITY 20

ST. LOUIS

LOUISVILLE 17

RICHMOND 31

SOUTH

Charleston

Savannah

NEW ORLEANS 12

St. Petersburg

after about 1900, there was a thinning out of the smallest service centers while larger centers with better access to enlarged market areas continued to grow.

Berry has also considered the relationship of the selective growth of service centers to the emergence of metropolitan or primate cities in a model which describes the transition from a region with a primate city and only small and sparsely distributed service centers to one with a more balanced rank-size distribution of settlements.[22] Occasionally specialized manufacturing or local resources stimulated the growth of intermediate-size towns, but most of them became part of the emerging hierarchy of service centers as the extensive and undifferentiated hinterland of the primate city was partitioned into smaller market areas. Friedmann has attempted to incorporate changes in city-size distribution into a model of regional economic development of newly settled areas.[23] He suggests that the spatial structure of these areas is dualistic, consisting of a highly urbanized "center" of intensive and diversified economic growth and an economically specialized and vulnerable "periphery" dependent on the center for its growth. Thus, because early settlement in the United States generally took place within an imperial political system, any newly settled area was a "periphery" of the economic "center" in Europe. A primate port monopolized the commercial and administrative functions of the colony, and towns in the interior were scattered and small. Political independence, improvements in inter-regional transportation, and local industrialization eventually enlarged the settled area and supported the growth of local "centers."

Perloff and Wingo have applied a similar "heartland-hinterland" model to the changing spatial structure of the American economy between 1840 and 1910.[24] They emphasize basic differences between the industrial heartland and the resource-based hinterland as well as striking contrasts in income distribution, level of economic specialization, and market relationships within the hinterland. Indeed, earlier Baldwin had argued that different productive functions may support quite different patterns and levels of economic development in newly settled areas with similar resources.[25] Clearly the regional economic specialization of a newly settled region strongly influenced initial patterns of urbanization and the rate at which a balanced city-size distribution emerged. For the United States, Williamson has indicated that regional levels of urbanization diverged between 1820 and 1860 but thereafter the differences gradually diminished.[26]

THE CHANGING REGIONAL PATTERN OF URBANIZATION

An elaboration of the urban dimension of these generalizations provides the basis of a model which describes the changing rates and locations of urbanization during the nineteenth century. This model attempts to identify the effects of differences in regional economic development on rates and levels of urban growth. Consequently, the aggregate results of economic change are necessarily emphasized, but at the expense of other considerations, often non-economic, which influenced the growth behavior of individual cities. It is hypothesized that urbanization in the United States between 1790 and 1910 responded to three basic changes in the spatial organization of the national economy:

1. The Establishment of the First Periphery
2. The Emergence of the Core in the Old Periphery and the Differentiation of the New Periphery
3. The Enlargement of the Core and the Integration of the New Periphery (Fig. 1-3)

1. *The Establishment of the First Periphery.* When North America was first settled, administrative and commercial centers were established to link the colonial peripheries with European centers. Almost without

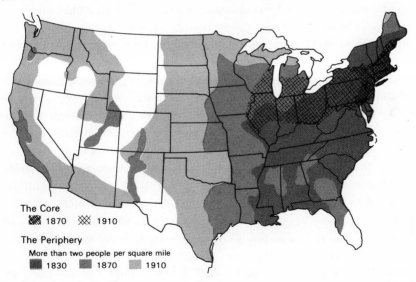

The Core
  ▓ 1870   ▒ 1910

The Periphery
More than two people per square mile
  ■ 1830   ■ 1870   ▨ 1910

FIG. 1-3. Changing Distribution of the Core and Periphery of the American Economy, 1830-1910

exception these urban beginnings were ports that controlled both the external commerce of the colony and the local supply needs of the settled area. Land transportation was difficult and expensive and, consequently, inland towns were small and few in number; most of the urban population was concentrated in a primate city. Because the commerce of an ideal colony consisted of exchanging staple exports for diverse manufactured goods produced in the mother country, the urban growth stimulated by this trade was largely concentrated in the ports of the economic core. Indeed, if locally produced staples were not channeled through a nascent port in the periphery then itinerant agents or factors tended to encourage the dispersal rather than the concentration of commercial activity. In contrast, inter-colonial trade, based upon the ability of the colonies to provide goods for one another that the mother country was reluctant or unable to provide, supported the growth of substantial primate cities and occasionally smaller ports as well.

2. *The Emergence of the Core in the Old Periphery and the Differentiation of the New Periphery.* With improvements in inland transportation, the periphery was greatly enlarged and selective industrialization in older settled areas created a discrete economic core within the limits of the former periphery. Clusters of towns of intermediate size emerged in the most intensely industrialized areas and also adjacent to the original primate cities. The transmission of people, capital, goods, and services into the new and expanding periphery sustained the growth not only of established ports within the core of the national economy but also of inland cities, which rapidly assumed leading positions in newly settled sections. These populous inland centers emerged at advantageous locations, first on the waterways, then on the railroad network, and, as in the first periphery, urban growth in some sections of the new periphery was compounded by the development of internal commerce. The largest cities were the main beneficiaries of this internal commerce, but during this phase a network of small service centers emerged to provide for local needs. The size and growth of these inland metropolises and the rate at which lower-order centers emerged within their hinterlands were in part dependent upon the kind of resource exploited and the degree of local economic diversification. The expanding railroad network greatly improved inter-regional transportation, but many resources within the periphery still lay beyond the reach of the early lines, and the exploitation of these resources awaited the development of an integrated national system.

3. *The Enlargement of the Core and the Integration of the New Periphery.* As selective industrialization proceeded, the originally small core of the national economy expanded into areas of the periphery containing resources and locations appropriate to the growth of manufacturing. Expansion of the railroads stimulated the rapid exploitation of formerly inaccessible resources and the growth of new inland cities which served the commercial needs of the newly settled sections of the periphery. During this phase, however, the rapid growth of metropolitan cities and the emergence of service centers within their hinterlands tended to diminish but not eliminate the striking regional differences in the initial urbanization of the periphery. In contrast, differences in the level of urbanization between the core and the periphery were maintained, for the continued industrialization of the enlarged core supported the growth of many populous cities.

THE ESTABLISHMENT OF THE FIRST PERIPHERY: URBANIZATION BEFORE 1830

The preceding model hypothesizes that urbanization within a newly settled periphery was restricted to primate port cities unless the commerce of the colony was diversified to include other sections of the periphery. During the colonial period the Southern, Middle Atlantic, and New England colonies made sharply contrasting adjustments to the potentialities and limitations of the English mercantile system; consequently, impressive regional variations in the level of urbanization developed. Although the American Revolution and the Napoleonic Wars disturbed colonial trade patterns and although some sections of the trans-Appalachian West were opened by about 1800, there were few major changes in patterns of urban growth before about 1830.

In 1790 the first United States census counted just under 4 million inhabitants. Only 5.1 per cent of the total population lived in settlements defined as urban by the Census Bureau (more than 2,500 people) and most of the urban dwellers were concentrated in the five towns with populations exceeding 10,000: Boston, New York, Philadelphia, Baltimore, and Charleston (Tables 1-1 and 1-2). Of the larger towns, all but Charleston were located on the northeastern seaboard between the Merrimack and Potomac rivers, but most of the smaller centers, such as Salem and Providence (each with about 5,000 people), were concentrated on the coast of New England (Fig. 1-4). Although there were no inland

TABLE 1-1
Growth of Settlements in the United States, 1790–1920

Number of Settlements with a Population of:
(by 1000's)

Year	One Million or More	500 to 1,000	250 to 500	100 to 250	50 to 100	25 to 50	10 to 25	2.5 to 10
1790						2	3	19
1800					1	2	3	27
1810					2	2	7	35
1820				1	2	2	8	48
1830				1	3	3	16	67
1840			1	2	2	7	25	94
1850		1	0	5	4	16	36	174
1860		2	1	6	7	19	58	299
1870		2	5	7	11	27	116	495
1880	1	3	4	12	15	42	146	715
1890	3	1	7	17	30	66	230	994
1900	3	3	9	23	40	82	280	1297
1910	3	5	11	31	59	119	369	1665
1920	3	9	13	43	76	143	465	1970

TABLE 1-2
Distribution of the Population in Settlements in the United States, 1790–1920

Per Cent of Total Population in Settlements with Populations of:
(by 1000's)

Year	One Million or More	500 to 1000	250 to 500	100 to 250	50 to 100	25 to 50	10 to 25	2.5 to 10	Under to 2.5
1790						1.6	1.2	2.3	94.9
1800					1.1	1.3	1.0	2.6	93.9
1810					2.1	1.1	1.5	2.6	92.7
1820				1.3	1.3	.7	1.3	2.6	92.8
1830				1.6	1.7	.8	1.9	2.8	91.2
1840			1.8	1.2	1.1	1.4	2.4	2.9	89.2
1850		2.2		2.8	1.2	2.6	2.4	3.9	84.7
1860		4.4	.9	3.2	1.4	2.1	2.8	5.0	80.2
1870		4.2	4.0	2.6	2.0	2.4	4.4	6.1	74.3
1880	2.4	3.8	2.6	3.6	1.9	2.9	4.4	6.6	71.8
1890	5.8	1.3	3.9	4.4	3.2	3.6	5.5	7.4	64.9
1900	8.5	2.2	3.8	4.3	3.6	3.7	5.7	8.0	60.3
1910	9.2	3.3	4.3	5.3	4.5	4.4	6.0	8.6	54.3
1920	9.6	5.9	4.3	6.2	5.0	4.8	6.7	8.8	48.8

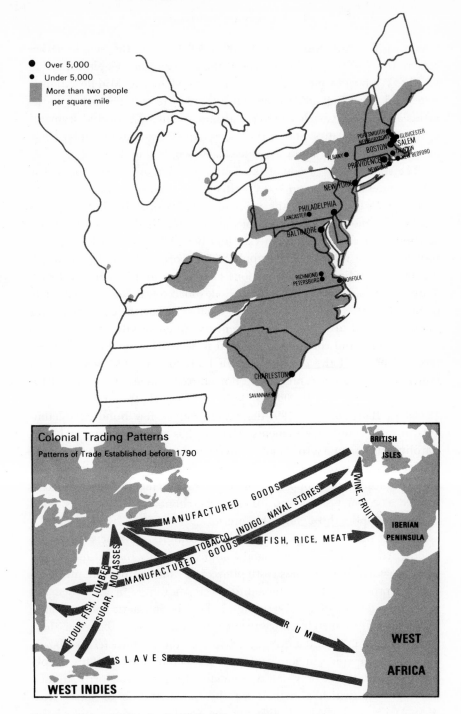

Over 5,000
Under 5,000
More than two people
per square mile

PORTSMOUTH
NEWBURYPORT   GLOUCESTER
BOSTON   SALEM
ALBANY   TAUNTON
PROVIDENCE   NEW BEDFORD
NEWPORT

NEW YORK

PHILADELPHIA
LANCASTER
BALTIMORE

RICHMOND   NORFOLK
PETERSBURG

CHARLESTON
SAVANNAH

Colonial Trading Patterns

Patterns of Trade Established before 1790

BRITISH
ISLES

MANUFACTURED GOODS

WINE, FRUIT

TOBACCO, INDIGO, NAVAL STORES

IBERIAN
PENINSULA

FISH, RICE, MEAT

MANUFACTURED GOODS

FLOUR, FISH, LUMBER
SUGAR, MOLASSES

R U M

WEST

S L A V E S

AFRICA

WEST INDIES

Fig. 1-4. Urbanization in the United States, 1790

towns with populations of more than 5,000, even the small market
centers which supplied the settlers in the interior and people departing
for the West were most heavily concentrated in the Middle Atlantic
states and New England. In the South there were very few urban settlements apart from Charleston and Baltimore which also served segments
of the Middle Atlantic States; these cities and Savannah, Norfolk, Richmond and Petersburg alone exceeded 2,500 people (Fig. 1-4).

The staple export trade of the Southern colonies had supported few
urban centers and the regional dominance of Charleston and Baltimore
in 1790 clearly illustrates the primate-port city-size distribution postu-
lated in the model. Charleston not only monopolized the export of rice
and indigo from coastal South Carolina but also established a regional
primacy in the more general supply and export trade of the surrounding area, including adjacent sections of Georgia and North Carolina.[27]
Throughout most of the colonial period, tobacco was consigned directly
to British ports from local wharves attached to coastal plantations but
toward the end of the eighteenth century, when production shifted to
the piedmont, and coastal areas turned to wheat production, Baltimore
rapidly engrossed the export trade in both tobacco and wheat.[28] Certainly smaller urban centers were not entirely absent from the settled
interior, but, whereas 16,000 people lived in Charleston and more than
13,000 in Baltimore in 1790, there were only a few hundred inhabitants in most interior settlements. Merrens has suggested that in North
Carolina rudimentary roads and waterways were adequate for local exchange but by about 1775 scarcely a dozen small centers existed.[29] Indeed, a substantial proportion of local trade remained highly decentralized as country stores and itinerant merchants from the larger ports
provided supplies throughout the interior.

Unlike the staples of the Southern colonies, products from the
Middle Atlantic and New England colonies had only limited markets in
Britain, which then had less costly sources of lumber, fur, fish, and agricultural produce. These commodities were, however, in great demand
in the plantations of the West Indies and the Southern colonies, and,
although British merchants controlled the direct trade between these
areas and the mother country, merchants of the northeastern seaboard
dominated the trade in foodstuffs and lumber products.[30] This supply
trade was, moreover, only one component of a complex North Atlantic
carrying trade which also included the transportation of slaves from
West Africa to the West Indies and the Southern colonies and of rice

and fish from North America to Southern Europe (Fig. 1-4). New England, with Boston in the lead, was the first section of the more northerly colonies to respond to the potential of the West Indian market, and by 1700 Boston had become the most populous town in North America, while a host of smaller ports had appeared along the coast from New Haven to Portsmouth. Once the process of urbanization had been initiated, shipbuilding and the manufacture of rum from imported molasses further stimulated the growth and multiplication of urban centers.

The response of the Middle Atlantic colonies to the plantation markets came somewhat later, largely because New York and Philadelphia and their backcountries began to develop rather later than New England. Yet, once the hinterlands of these cities had been settled, their productivity in wheat and meat products gave them substantial advantages over the ports of New England. Furthermore, trade in the Middle Atlantic colonies was heavily concentrated in New York and Philadelphia whereas in New England, where fish rather than agricultural produce provided a leading export cargo, it was divided amongst a dozen or so ports (Fig. 1-4). Rapid settlement, and productive exploitation in southeastern Pennsylvania especially, gave Philadelphia merchants a secure medium of exchange in the Southern colonies and in the West Indies and Southern Europe, and by about 1750 Philadelphia had a greater population than Boston. New York similarly outgrew Boston, but remained second in rank to Philadelphia until after the Revolution. The regional dominance of New York and Philadelphia not only inhibited the growth of smaller ports but also of inland towns. Lemon has suggested that Philadelphia engrossed the retail and buying functions of potential lower-order centers because the larger scale of business organization yielded substantial cost advantages in local trade.[31] Similarly, the local trade of the backcountry was concentrated in a limited number of county seats and the intervening areas supported very few lower-order centers. Agricultural development in the Middle Atlantic colonies was actually more conducive to the growth of inland towns than it was in the South. Yet because Philadelphia and New York were much larger than either Charleston or Baltimore, their primacy was quite as impressive as that of the southern ports .

Between 1790 and 1830 the Atlantic ports maintained their regional primacy, and with the purchase of the Louisiana Territory in 1803 the United States gained an additional primate port, New Orleans. In the same period, the population of the new country increased fourfold to about 12.9 million people. The population of the ninety settlements with more than 2,500 people increased eight times and accounted for almost 9 per cent of the total population (Tables 1-1 and 1-2). In absolute terms the majority of the new urban residents lived in the four northeastern seaports—Boston, New York, Philadelphia, and Baltimore—the four largest cities of the Union and the only settlements with more than 50,000 inhabitants. Together, these cities contained almost 40 per cent of the total urban population while New York City alone, with a population of more than 200,000, accounted for almost 20 per cent.

During the Napoleonic Wars the demand for American produce and re-exports increased sharply and the major northeastern seaports enjoyed almost two decades of rapid expansion. With the Jeffersonian Embargo on trade in 1807 and, more particularly with the termination of the Napoleonic Wars in 1815, American dependence upon diverse foreign markets declined and the major seaports gradually turned their attention to domestic markets and to the development of commerce with the expanding western and southern frontiers.[32] Cotton rapidly replaced wheat and flour as the leading exports of the United States while Britain, the leading market for the staple fiber, also provided the bulk of American imported goods.

The most impressive result of changing trade patterns was New York's rise to undisputed national primacy. By 1830, the population of the city was more than 200,000 and the adjacent settlements of Brooklyn and Newark had more than 15,000 and 10,000 inhabitants, respectively. New York had better access to the continental interior through the Hudson Valley and the Mohawk Gap than any of its three rival ports, yet control of the external trade of the South rather than direct export of surplus goods from its own hinterland gave the city its initial commercial supremacy. To be sure, the Erie Canal was completed in 1825 but it tended to serve the increasingly well settled areas of upstate New York rather than the through traffic of the sparsely settled upper sections of the Middle West. Upstate New York was one of the few interior parts of the United States where urbanization had even modest beginnings. Albany, with more than 24,000 people, was the second largest inland town in the nation, Troy had a population of more than 10,000 and Rochester, Buffalo, and Utica all exceeded 8,000 (Fig. 1-5).

Albion attributes the spectacular growth of New York City in these forty years to the expansion of trade between Britain and the United States rather than to the export of western staples, which did not move

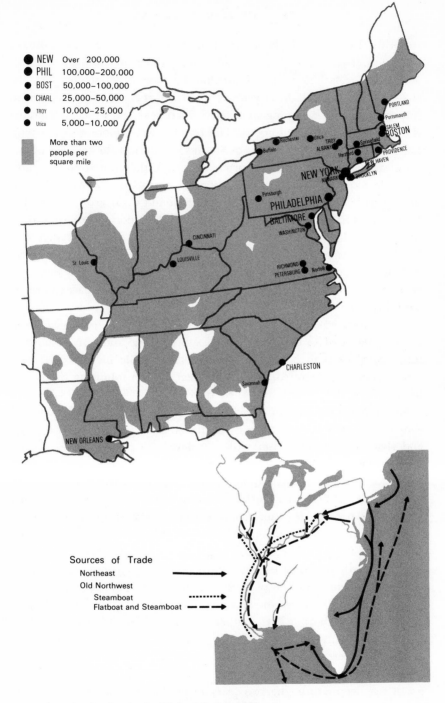

Legend from map:

● NEW — Over 200,000
● PHIL — 100,000–200,000
● BOST — 50,000–100,000
● CHARL — 25,000–50,000
● TROY — 10,000–25,000
● Utica — 5,000–10,000

More than two people per square mile

Map labels:

PORTLAND
Portsmouth
SALEM
BOSTON
Rochester
Utica
TROY
Springfield
Buffalo
ALBANY
Hartford
PROVIDENCE
NEW HAVEN
NEW YORK
NEWARK
BROOKLYN
Pittsburgh
PHILADELPHIA
BALTIMORE
WASHINGTON
CINCINNATI
St. Louis
LOUISVILLE
RICHMOND
PETERSBURG
Norfolk
CHARLESTON
Savannah
NEW ORLEANS

Sources of Trade
Northeast
Old Northwest
Steamboat
Flatboat and Steamboat

FIG. 1-5. Urbanization in the United States, 1830

down the Erie Canal in large quantities until the 1840's.[33] Even during the colonial period New York had maintained closer and more direct commercial relations with Britain than had any other major port. Between 1815 and 1830, the city greatly increased its position in the British import trade by developing an effective auction system which accelerated the sale and turnover of goods. The imports were, moreover, partly financed by direct consignments of Southern cotton to the textile mills of southeast Lancashire. The exporters of cotton, the United States's most valuable export before the Civil War, came to rely on New York as heavily as tobacco producers from the South and sugar growers from the West Indies had relied on all of the northeastern ports during the colonial period. The regulations of the old colonial commercial system had discouraged American participation in the movement of staples directly to Britain from the areas of primary production but, during the early nineteenth century, American ports, New York in particular, embraced even this trade.

In contrast, Boston, Philadelphia, and Baltimore had been more firmly committed to the carrying and supply trade and were somewhat less responsive than New York to the considerable increase in direct trade between the United States and Great Britain following the Napoleonic Wars. Baltimore established reasonably profitable trans-Atlantic connections on the basis of tobacco exports to the German states, and its commercial growth was even greater than that of its northern neighbor and rival, Philadelphia. But with the development of manufacturing, Philadelphia experienced a vigorous population growth and in 1830 still had twice as many people.[34] After the construction of the Erie Canal, Philadelphia and Baltimore competed to build similar systems across the Appalachians; thus, competition for western markets was well started before the development of railroads. Boston also directed surplus commercial funds into manufacturing—but within its immediate hinterland rather than within its own limits. To further commercial expansion, the city continued to pioneer new sources of carrying trade in the Pacific[35] and concentrated the far-flung trade of the smaller New England ports in its own harbor. Yet southern New England still remained one of the most highly urbanized sections of the United States; Salem, Providence, and New Haven each had a population of more than 10,000 (Fig. 1-5).

In the deep South, the two primate ports were less populous than those of the northeastern seaboard. Nevertheless, Charleston was the sixth largest city in the Union with more than 30,000 inhabitants and New Orleans was fifth with more than 43,000. Baltimore served a considerable section of the upper South, but the diversity of its trade closely resembled that of the northeastern cities, although the port handled very little of the South's new staple, cotton. Indeed, it was largely because the merchants of New York and their itinerant factors controlled the cotton trade that urbanization in the South was extremely slow. Even the growth of New Orleans was partly based upon the export of commodities from the Ohio Valley. As in upstate New York, a navigable river system encouraged early settlement and commercial development in the Old Northwest, but the Ohio-Mississippi system provided a circuitous route by rivers and coastal waters to eastern markets, and the early urban centers were primarily concerned with the supply trade for westward-moving settlers (Fig. 1-5). Until steamboats made upstream traffic possible, urban life in the Ohio Valley was sustained by a circular pattern of inter-regional trade which comprised overland movements of manufactured goods from the east to the Old Northwest, the downstream movement of agricultural produce to New Orleans, and finally the coastal movement of these goods to northeastern cities or to the West Indies.[36] Some of this produce may also have found its way into Southern markets either directly by way of the southern tributaries of the Ohio, or indirectly by way of New Orleans, but the food deficits of cotton-producing areas were not substantial before 1830.

Although the inter-regional linkages between the western frontier and the northeast were circuitous, in 1830 Cincinnati was already the largest inland city in the United States with a population of almost 25,000 and Pittsburgh and Louisville each had about half that number (Fig. 1-5). As in the canalized river system of upstate New York, local urbanization was well started, but rapid commercial development and urbanization awaited not only internal improvements, but also an increase in the European demand for wheat and the settlement of rich agricultural sections of the Middle West. Even though the two major inland regions of urbanization in the Ohio Valley and upstate New York together contained about 15 per cent of the total population resident in settlements with more than 10,000 people in 1830, the major urban development of the early nineteenth century was the consolidation of the urban primacy of the northeastern ports.

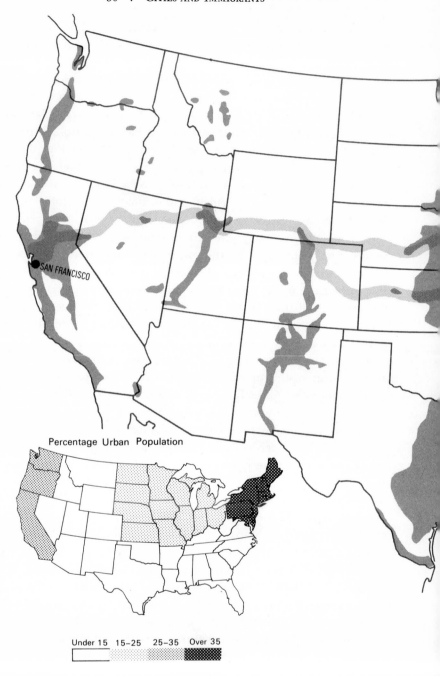

FIG. 1-6. Urbanization in the United States, 1870

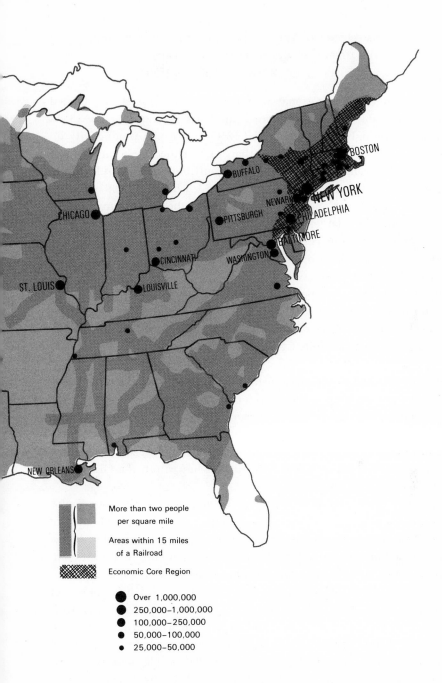

More than two people
per square mile

Areas within 15 miles
of a Railroad

Economic Core Region

Over 1,000,000
250,000–1,000,000
100,000–250,000
50,000–100,000
25,000–50,000

THE EMERGENCE OF THE CORE IN THE OLD PERIPHERY AND
THE DIFFERENTIATION OF THE NEW PERIPHERY:
URBANIZATION BETWEEN 1830 AND 1870

Although the international industrial preeminence of the United
States was established primarily after the Civil War, during the 1830's
and more strikingly in the 1840's and 1850's, per capita productivity increased at a rate somewhat greater than that of the long-term trend of
the nineteenth century. In addition, the contribution of manufacturing
to the total commercial product almost doubled between 1839 and 1859
to account for almost one third of the total at the latter date.[37] Manufacturing increased largely in the older settled areas, which formed a
new regional economic core within the limits of the former periphery.
Almost one half of the people in these areas lived in cities, and, although
most of the urban population was still located in long established pri-
mate-ports, a substantial portion was to be found in clusters of towns of
intermediate size. Productivity was also increased through settlement of
the expanding periphery of the continental interior, where there were
new resources to be exploited. At first this area was served by a few large
centers, and the collection and export of products from the periphery
were concentrated in towns strategically located on the emerging inter-
regional transportation system. Cities of intermediate size tended to appear more slowly there, but a network of smaller urban centers did
emerge with the gradual diversification of local economic activity. Yet
the rate and timing of these urban developments were not only quite
different between South and Old Northwest but within the Old Northwest as well.

Between 1830 and 1870 the areas in and around the four major
northeastern seaports and sections of southern New England, upstate
New York, and southeastern Pennsylvania supported a sizeable industrial production and formed the center of the expanding American economy (Fig. 1-6). By 1870 almost 60 per cent of the urban population of the
United States lived in New England and the Middle Atlantic states, and
more than 40 per cent of the region's total population (as compared with
20 per cent for the country as a whole) lived in settlements with more
than 2500 people (Table 1-3). Each of the four long-dominant primate-
ports in the Northeast had more than 250,000 people, and almost all
towns with populations between 25,000 and 100,000 were concentrated

TABLE 1-3

Distribution of the Urban Population of the United States, 1870

	Per Cent Urban	Per Cent U. S. Urban	Number of Cities with Populations of: (by 1000's)					Total
			500 to 1000	250 to 500	100 to 250	50 to 100	25 to 50	
New England	44.4	15.5		1		2	9	12
Middle Atlantic1	44.1	43.4	2	2	3	5	6	18
Great Lakes	21.6	19.7		1	1	3	4	9
South East	9.5	11.0			2	1	5	8
Plains	18.9	7.3	1				1	2
South West	6.9	0.7					1	1
Mountain	13.9	0.2						0
Far West	31.2	2.2			1		1	2
United States	20.9	100.0	2	5	7	11	27	52

1. Buffalo and Pittsburgh are included in the statistics for the Middle Atlantic Region but their growth characteristics more closely resembled those of cities in the Great Lakes Region. Brooklyn and Allegheny are counted as separate cities.

Note: For boundaries see Fig. 1-6.

in the same part of the country. Of some thirty-eight settlements with between 25,000 and 100,000 people, no fewer than twenty-two were in southern New England, New York and Pennsylvania. In addition to the growth of manufacturing centers, other settlements expanded rapidly on the margins of or between the large seaports. Brooklyn, for example, was the third most populous city in the nation in 1870. To the south of New York City, Newark had passed 100,000 and Jersey City had more than 80,000. The growth of cities adjacent to Boston was less impressive, but Cambridge and Charleston had populations of 39,000 and 28,000 respectively.

Within settled sections of the periphery, Chicago and St. Louis each had more than 250,000 people in 1870 and were ranked fourth and fifth among American cities. Cincinnati was ranked eighth with more than 200,000 people. Until about 1850 those parts of the Old Northwest adjacent to the Ohio-Mississippi river system grew most rapidly, but by 1870 cities on the Great Lakes had equalled the performances of the river cities to the south. In 1850 Cincinnati was still the largest inland city with a population of more than 115,000 and St. Louis had more than 75,000 inhabitants, but Chicago, Detroit, and Cleveland each contained fewer than 30,000. This variable growth was based primarily on the development of effective steamboat services and on the early settlement of the lower section of the Middle West between Cincinnati and St. Louis. Although steamboats had been introduced on the Ohio-Mississippi system as early as 1811, it was during the 1830's and 1840's that regular services increased the volume of trade between New Orleans and the growing river towns.[38] Cincinnati and to a lesser degree Pittsburgh and Louisville were the first inland centers to benefit from the more effective export linkage with New Orleans and from the receipts of imports transported upstream rather than overland from the east. But as the limit of settlement shifted westward and as sections of the bottom-lands of the middle Mississippi and Illinois valleys were cultivated, the river commerce of St. Louis exceeded that of towns on the Ohio. Direct trade between the Old Northwest and the cotton-producing areas of the South was also encouraged by the steamboat services, but the magnitude and complexity of this inter-regional commerce remains controversial.[39]

Although steamboats lowered transportation costs between New Orleans and the Old Northwest, export connections between the Ohio Valley and the Northeast still involved a roundabout route, and until canals and railroads increased the volume of eastbound traffic, river towns must

FIG. 1-7. Major Canals in the Northeastern United States, 1850

have benefitted heavily from supplying settlers and organizing the import trade. The first effort to improve export routes to the Northeast was the construction of a system of canals which linked the Ohio-Mississippi river system to the Great Lakes and the Erie Canal. By 1860 about 4250 miles of canals connected the various tributaries of the great natural waterways of the United States.[40] But the system was never well integrated and because of railroad competition only a limited number of the canals were commercially successful[41] (Fig. 1-7).

The eastern sections of the Old Northwest benefitted most from the canal network, and, although the Great Lakes waterway provided a good connection to eastern markets, the settlement and agricultural specialization of Illinois, southern Michigan and Wisconsin, and eastern Iowa awaited the more certain markets of the 1850's and the development of the steel plow, barbed wire, and partly mechanized harvesting equipment.[42] A further stimulus to production in the Middle West was the construction of the first inter-regional railroad system in the 1850's. Until that time the railroad "network" was little more than a group of small and generally unconnected passenger-focused routes, but by the outbreak of the Civil War a system covering more than 30,000 miles had been built (Fig. 1-8). The contest for freight traffic was more prolonged than for passenger traffic, and, although canal tonnage was almost double the amount moved by rail in 1852, railroads had attained a dominant place in freight movements by 1860.[43]

The social and economic benefits of the heavy investments in nineteenth-century canal and railroad construction recently have aroused considerable interest. Although settlement of new land unquestionably enlarged markets and contributed to increased per capita productivity, similar increments well might have been possible within long-settled areas had the transportation investment been diverted to increasing the efficiency of production.[44] The investment in transportation might have been considered high from the perspective of the national economy; nevertheless, in the newly settled West, it decidedly accelerated economic growth. The relationship between railroads and urbanization, however, was neither direct nor simple.[45] Chicago, it is true, excelled St. Louis in railroad enterprise, and by 1870 almost equalled the older city in population. Between 1850 and 1870, St. Louis, already committed to investments in steamboat services and overly confident of eastern railroad connections, concentrated on developing a trans-continental line at a time when Chicago was rapidly extending railroads in the western

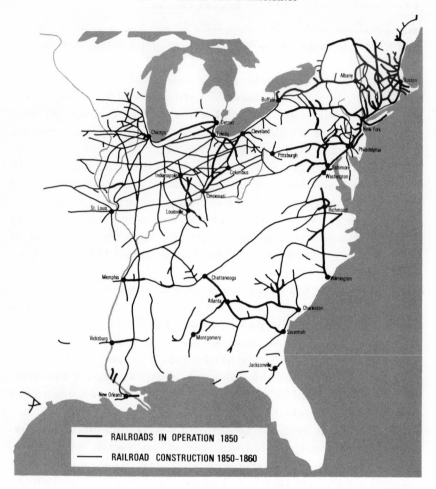

Fig. 1-8. Railroad Expansion in the United States, 1850-1860

fringes of the agricultural Middle West, including areas well within the adjacent hinterland of St. Louis.[46]

By about 1870, however, there were very few areas in the Middle West without effective rail connections to the Northeast (Fig. 1-6). The rapid growth of Chicago as the leading export assembler for agricultural products and as the leading distributor of imported manufactured goods was based in part on effective credit connections. Eastern capital not only financed the construction of railroads across Iowa, Missouri, Wisconsin, and Minnesota but apparently was responsible for the development of the city as a marketing and exchange center. The railroads were merely the instruments of a basic economic nexus which linked Chicago with New York and other eastern sources of capital more closely than any other Middle Western city.

The re-orientation of inter-regional trade from the Ohio-Mississippi system to the railroads and waterways linking the Middle West with northeastern seaports also stimulated the growth of several other large cities on the Great Lakes. By 1870 Cleveland, Detroit, and Milwaukee all had exceeded 70,000, and Buffalo had a population of more than 100,000. The river cities of the southern sections of the Middle West not only faced the problem of adjusting to the new inter-regional trade but also suffered severely when their southern markets were dislocated during and after the Civil War. Nevertheless, railroad connections with the East maintained the commercial growth of the larger river towns and Cincinnati, in particular, remained a major inland metropolis, monopolizing most of the external commerce of its hinterland.

Indeed, irrespective of major differences in the timing and rate of urbanization in the Old Northwest, cities which in 1870 had more than about 70,000 people collectively monopolized the external commercial relations of the entire region. St. Louis (310,864), Chicago (298,977), and Cincinnati (216,239) controlled large hinterlands, while cities with populations between 70,000 and 200,000 served smaller sub-regions. Few cities with populations between 20,000 and 70,000 existed. In 1870 the trans-Appalachian interior north of the Ohio had three cities with more than 200,000 people and nine with more than 70,000, but only five in the range between 20,000 and 70,000. Grain production required numerous but relatively small marketing and service centers and the rapid expansion and increased density of railroads encouraged a highly decentralized commercial organization.[47] Interchangeable mechanical parts were dispatched by producers to local stations, and elevators and warehouses were provided at quite frequent intervals on most railroads. Although the external commerce of the staple-producing periphery demanded the services of several large metropolitan centers, service at the local level was provided by extremely small centers. Consequently, the emerging urban hierarchy was characterized by unusually large proportions of both large and small urban centers.

The urban characteristics of the Old Northwest in 1870 were quite different from those of the South where metropolitan cities were fewer and smaller and where lower-order centers had scarcely emerged at all. Although in 1870 New Orleans had almost 200,000 people and was, like the river cities of the upper Ohio, a major center of inter-regional trade, its dimensions and functions were more limited than those of the largest Middle Western cities. Still, the city was the only large metropolitan center serving the deep South, and, of the five other Southern cities with populations of more than 25,000, only Richmond (51,000) exceeded 50,000. Indeed, three of the five—Charleston, Savannah, and Mobile—were ports and a fourth, Memphis, was a river town. But apparently these small cities served the entire urban needs of the South for evidence of local urbanization in the form of an expanding network of small service centers was extremely limited.

The lack of a strong urban response to the regional economic specialization of the South has been related to the limited mechanical services required by cotton production and to the limited differentiation of intermediate stages between production and final marketing. In the grain-producing areas of the Old Northwest elaborate storage facilities were needed to preserve quality, and effective supply trades were essential to maintain increasing mechanization. In addition, collection and marketing was divided into several segments—from elevator storage to consignment to purchasers. The marketing of cotton, however, became highly concentrated in the hands of itinerant factors or agents who provided the entire range of commercial services. Moreover, the staple cotton areas were confined to a limited section of the Southern states. The remaining areas were not only more sparsely settled but also had developed only fragmentary and ephemeral external commerce. Their markets were largely local and commodity transfers demanded no elaborate commercial infra-structure. The South has been described as a dual economy in which the commercial sector was spatially limited, but, since even this sector relied very heavily on direct and undifferentiated commercial links with the center, local urban growth was slow.[48]

In 1870 the Great Plains and Far West were largely unsettled and the first transcontinental railroad was barely two years old. Apart from early concentrations of miners and several well separated centers of settlement on the Pacific coast, the area west of the hundredth meridian was incorporated into the periphery during the last three decades of the nineteenth century. Only San Francisco with a population just under 150,000 provided external connections between the developed parts of the Far West and the center of the American economy, and in this function the port was unrivalled. No other settlement in that area exceeded 25,000 people.

THE ENLARGEMENT OF THE CORE AND THE INTEGRATION
OF THE NEW PERIPHERY: URBANIZATION BETWEEN 1870 AND 1910

In the third phase of development, the small economic core incorporated adjacent industrialized sections, and a newly completed continental transportation system stimulated the enlargement and metropolitan organization of the new periphery. Eventually, between one half and three quarters of the total population lived in urban settlements within the enlarged core, many of them cities with more than 250,000 people. All of these cities served at least some of the needs of their adjacent hinterlands, and most of them also produced manufactured products for national and international markets. Although the expansion of the periphery was accompanied by the early establishment of metropolitan cities and the subdivision of their hinterlands by smaller centers, obvious if diminishing regional variations in urbanization remained. By 1910 for example, most of the present metropolitan centers of the United States had established the basis of their current regional dominance, but in some areas, particularly in the South and Southwest, the future metropolises had small populations and their hinterlands had attained only a low level of urbanization. Indeed between 1870 and 1910, industrial growth within the center of the American economy created many more populous cities than did metropolitan growth within the periphery.

In 1870 more than half of both the country's urban population and the fourteen settlements with populations exceeding 100,000 were located in New England and the Middle Atlantic states. Between 1870 and 1910, these areas maintained a vigorous rate of urbanization, and by 1910 almost three quarters of their populations were urban (Table 1-4). Meanwhile, the industrialization of the western parts of the Middle Atlantic region and of the Great Lakes region resulted in a major westward expansion of the center of the economy and the fast growth of several interior cities.[49] In 1870 when slightly more than 21 per cent of the national labor force were employed in manufacturing, only New England with 44 per cent and the Middle Atlantic states with 32 per cent exceeded this national average. By 1890 the Great Lakes states had also exceeded the average, but with the exception of the Far Western states, the other regions had relatively low proportions of people employed in manufacturing (Table 1-5). Accordingly, the newly enlarged industrial center which, by 1910, occupied most sections of the Northeastern and

TABLE 1-4

Regional Distribution of the Urban Population of the United States, 1910

	Per Cent Urban	Per Cent U. S. Urban	Number of Cities with Populations Greater Than: (by 1000's)					
			1000 or More	500 to 1000	250 to 500	100 to 250	50 to 100	Total
New England	73.3	11.4		1		7	12	20
Middle Atlantic	70.2	35.3	2	2	4	5	18	31
Great Lakes	52.7	22.9	1	1	3	5	11	21
South East	19.4	10.2			1	6	6	13
Plains	33.2	9.2		1	1	3	5	10
South West	22.5	3.3					5	5
Mountain	40.7	2.0				1	1	2
Far West	56.0	5.7			2	4	1	7
United States	45.7	100.0	3	5	11	31	59	109

Note: For boundaries see Fig. 1-9.

TABLE 1-5

Proportions of the Total Labor Force Employed in Manufacturing by Regions, 1870–1910

	Per Cent of Total		
	1870	1890	1910
New England	44.1	47.9	49.1
Middle Atlantic	32.1	35.8	39.8
Great Lakes	19.7	25.0	33.2
Plains	14.9	16.4	20.0
Mountains	12.9	20.0	20.5
Far West	18.2	22.6	27.0
South East	7.5	10.5	14.5
South West	7.0	9.1	12.4
United States	21.1	24.3	27.9

From H. Perloff, et. al., *Regions, Resources and Economic Growth,* Baltimore, 1960, pp. 172-83.

Note: For boundaries see Fig. 1-9.

Great Lakes states, was subsequently identified as the American Manufacturing Belt.

In 1910 the Manufacturing Belt supported no fewer than thirty-four of the fifty cities with more than 100,000 people and fourteen of the nineteen cities with more than 250,000 inhabitants (Fig. 1-9). At least seven of these centers were commercial metropolises before 1870, but most of the others had increased their numbers as manufacturing expanded, and often in locations with decidedly limited potential for metropolitan dominance. Cleveland, Pittsburgh, and Detroit, in particular, exhibited extremely high rates of growth. In 1870 not one of the three cities had a population of more than 100,000, but by 1910 Cleveland and Pittsburgh were the sixth and eighth most populous cities in the nation, each with more than 450,000 inhabitants. The basic industrial cities also provided semi-finished materials, so that medium-sized manufacturing towns were numerous throughout the enlarged center. Of about fifty-nine cities with populations between 50,000 and 100,000 in 1910, forty-two were located in the Manufacturing Belt. Many of them provided local services but the majority were dependent on manufacturing and needed a national market to support their increasing populations.

Regional differences in the proportion of the total labor force in the

TABLE 1-6

Proportions of the Total Labor Force Employed in Services by Regions, 1870–1910

	Per Cent of Total		
	1870	1890	1910
New England	28.0	34.2	40.3
Middle Atlantic	36.4	42.1	45.6
Great Lakes	23.1	32.6	38.6
Plains	22.7	30.4	37.0
Mountain	26.1	39.6	40.4
Far West	36.0	41.3	47.6
South East	16.8	21.6	24.0
South West	18.8	25.5	27.8
United States	25.4	32.3	36.5

From H. Perloff, et. al., *Regions, Resources and Economic Growth,* Baltimore, 1960, pp. 172-83.

Note: For boundaries see Fig. 1-9.

Percentage Urban Population

Under 30   30–50   50–70   Over 70

FIG. 1-9. Urbanization in the United States, 1910

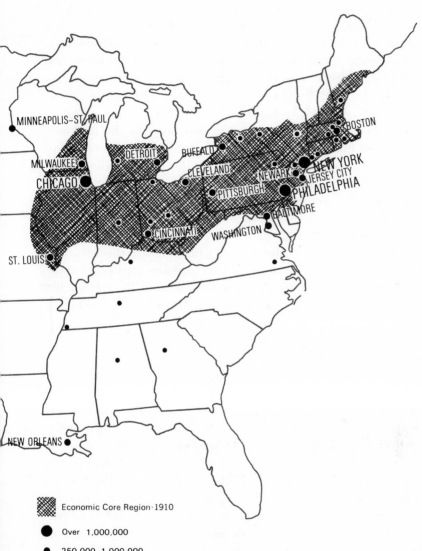

Economic Core Region·1910

● Over 1,000,000

● 250,000–1,000,000

• 100,000– 250,000

service sector were less evident than those in manufacturing, for the cities in the periphery supported as rapid an expansion of service employment as in most parts of the core. Although high proportions of the populations of New England and the Middle Atlantic and Great Lakes states continued to be employed in service industries, by 1910 the level of service employment in the Plains, Mountain, and particularly the Pacific states was higher than in the core region and the nation as a whole (Table 1-6). In 1870 the western states were either sparsely populated or unsettled, and San Francisco, St. Louis, and Portland provided most of the commercial services needed in that vast area. By 1910 continental railroads linked most of the West with the domestic and industrial markets of the Middle West and the Northeast, and, although the major metropolitan centers relied on these ties, the relationship between railroad construction and metropolitan growth was complicated by the ability of several prominent centers to survive and grow without rail service.[50] Kansas City, Denver, and Seattle were initially ignored by transcontinental routes and subsequently gained service through community enterprise based upon an established preeminence in the supply trade for local resources. Once the railroads extended throughout the western states, the presence of abundant resources continued to influence local urbanization, the fastest growth occurring on the Pacific coast where resources were most plentiful. San Francisco was the most populous western city in 1910, but Los Angeles already had more than 250,000 people and Seattle and Portland each supported more than 200,000 inhabitants. More than one half of all people in the three Pacific states were urban residents, and with the development of manufacturing several of the area's metropolitan centers assumed the characteristics of the center rather than of the periphery of the American economy.

Interior sections of the West supported fewer cities because of the extent of grain farming and cattle ranching. Thus, only one third of the population of the Plains states and about 40 per cent of the Mountain states were urban dwellers (Table 1-4). In 1870 St. Louis and San Francisco monopolized commerce in the western interior, but by 1910 Minneapolis-St. Paul with more than 500,000 people, Kansas City and Denver with more than 200,000, and Omaha with more than 100,000 controlled the supply and marketing activities of extensive hinterlands. The Mountain and Southwestern states supported rather smaller metropolitan centers and in the Southwest no one city had established metropolitan primacy. Although Dallas, Houston, and San Antonio all exceeded 75,000 in population, only 22 per cent of the total population of the Southwest were urban (Table 1-4). Urbanization and metropolitan growth in this section of the country took place at least a generation later than in the northern and central Plains or the Pacific Coast.

The lowest rate of urbanization in the country during the years 1870 to 1910 was in the South, where as late as 1910 less than 20 per cent of the popualtion were city dwellers (Table 1-4). In 1870 New Orleans and Louisville were the most populous cities in the Southeastern states, their preeminence relating to commercial connections with the Old Northwest. In 1910 New Orleans was the only southern city with more than 250,000 people, but, because of the more spectacular growth of northern and western cities, this eighth most populous city in 1870 had become the fifteenth in 1910. The second most populous city in 1910 was Louisville, which like Cincinnati and St. Louis served both the lower Middle West and the South. It too experienced a decline in rank. In 1870 Nashville, Memphis and Richmond were the largest cities in each of their areas, but all still maintained local preeminence in 1910, with populations ranging between 110,000 and 131,000. The most spectacular growth among southern cities was in Birmingham, where industry had started to develop, and in Atlanta, which had already established a metropolitan dominance in the surrounding area. Yet, in 1910 there were still only 154,000 people in Atlanta and 132,000 in Birmingham. Clearly their size was modest compared to northern industrial cities and western metropolitan centers. Even before the Civil War, the commercial needs of the South had generated very few urban centers, and economic difficulties and a low rate of economic growth in the Southeast provided few additional stimulants to urbanization.[51]

In 1910 metropolitan organization in some parts of the periphery was incomplete and there was considerable variation in the area as a whole. Moreover, after 1910 the increased use of petroleum and natural gas energy, advances in the petro-chemical and communications industries, and the development of long-distance road and air transportation strongly influenced selective metropolitan growth and differences in rates of economic development. Although the size and growth rates of different centers have varied widely over the past sixty years, almost all of the cities that had established industrial preeminence or metropolitan dominance by 1900 maintain their high ranks today.

This discussion has been largely concerned with the emergence of major cities and with regional differences in the level of urbanization that were related to the changing spatial structure of the national economy. Nineteenth-century urbanization, however, was affected by the selective growth of a hierarchy of lower-order service centers, and the dynamics of metropolitan growth has hitherto attracted considerably more attention than has the evolving system of service centers within their hinterlands. Theoretical considerations of the settlement hierarchy have been concerned primarily with the functional and behavioral basis of regularities in the location of service centers but their developmental implications have not been fully explored. For these reasons this chapter has attempted to describe the location of industrial and metropolitan urban growth and variations and convergences in regional urbanization rather than the more universal spatial characteristics displayed by settlements of a lower rank and order. Like all "stage" or "phase" schemes of development the suggested chronological limits of the model are approximations, for the transition from one period to another frequently extended over a decade or more.

NOTES

1. E. E. Lampard, "The History of Cities in the Economically Advanced Areas," *Economic Development and Cultural Change,* 3, 1955, pp. 81-136.
2. F. J. Turner, "The Significance of the Frontier in American History," *Proceedings of the State Historical Society of Wisconsin,* 41, 1894, pp. 79-112; F. Mood, "Studies in the History of American Settled Areas and Frontier Lines, 1625-1790," *Agricultural History,* 26, 1952, pp. 16-34.
3. N. S. B. Gras, *An Introduction to Economic History,* New York, 1922.
4. J. Rubin, "Urban Growth and Development," in D. T. Gilchrist, ed., *The Growth of Seaport Cities: 1790-1825,* Charlottesville, 1967, pp. 3-21; J. M. S. Careless, "Frontierism, Metropolitanism and Canadian History," *Canadian Historical Review,* 35, 1954, pp. 1-21.
5. R. C. Wade, *The Urban Frontier,* Cambridge, 1959, pp. 1-71; C. M. Gates, "The Role of Cities in the Westward Movement," *Mississippi Valley Historical Review,* 37, 1950, pp. 277-78.
6. D. C. North, *The Economic Growth of the United States, 1790-1860,* Englewood Cliffs, N.J., 1961.
7. E. Smolensky and D. Ratejczak, "The Conception of Cities," *Explorations in Entrepreneurial History,* 2nd Series, 2, 1965, pp. 90-131.
8. J. Rubin, *op. cit.,* pp. 3-21.
9. H. S. Perloff, et. al., *Regions, Resources and Economic Growth,* Baltimore, 1960, pp. 57-59.

10. W. R. Thompson, *A Preface to Urban Economics,* Baltimore, 1965, pp. 15-16.
11. *Ibid.,* p. 17.
12. A. R. Pred, "Industrialization, Initial Advantage and American Metropolitan Growth," *Geographical Review,* 55, 1965, pp. 158-85 and *The Spatial Dynamics of U.S. Urban-Industrial Growth, 1800-1914: Interpretative and Theoretical Essays,* Cambridge, 1966, pp. 24-39 and 177-85.
13. J. R. Borchert, "American Metropolitan Evolution," *Geographical Review,* 57, 1967, pp. 301-32.
14. E. E. Lampard, "The Evolving System of Cities in the United States: Urbanization and Economic Development," in H. S. Perloff and L. Wingo, eds., *Issues in Urban Economics,* Baltimore, 1968, pp. 81-138.
15. C. H. Madden, "On Some Indicators of Stability in the Growth of Cities in the United States," *Economic Development and Cultural Change,* 4, 1955-56, pp. 236-52.
16. F. Lukermann, "Empirical Expressions of Nodality and Hierarchy in a Circulation Manifold," *East Lakes Geographer,* 2, 1966, pp. 17-44.
17. F. Lukermann, *op. cit.,* p. 29.
18. J. G. Williamson and J. A. Swanson, "The Growth of Cities in the American North East, 1820-1920," *Explorations in Entrepreneurial History,* 2nd Series, 4, 1966, supplement.
19. R. Higgs, "The Growth of Cities in a Midwestern Region, 1870-1900," *Journal of Regional Science,* 9, 1969, pp. 369-75.
20. W. Christaller, *The Central Places of Southern Germany,* C. Baskin, trans., Englewood Cliffs, N.J., 1966.
21. B. J. L. Berry, *Geography of Market Centers and Retail Distribution,* Englewood Cliffs, N.J., 1967, pp. 5-9.
22. B. J. L. Berry, "City Size Distribution and Economic Development," *Economic Development and Cultural Change,* 9, 1961, pp. 573-88.
23. J. Friedmann, "Regional Economic Policy for Developing Areas," *Papers and Proceedings of the Regional Science Association,* 11, 1963, pp. 41-61.
24. H. S. Perloff and L. Wingo, Jr., "Natural Resource Endowment and Regional Economic Growth," in J. J. Spengler, ed., *Natural Resources and Economic Growth,* Washington, D.C., 1961, pp. 191-212.
25. R. Baldwin, "Patterns of Development in Newly Settled Regions," *Manchester School of Economic and Social Studies,* 24, 1956, pp. 161-79.
26. J. G. Williamson, "Antebellum Urbanization in the American Northeast," *Journal of Economic History,* 25, 1965, pp. 592-608.
27. C. Bridenbaugh, *Cities in Revolt, Urban Life in America, 1743-1776,* New York, 1955, pp. 261-62.
28. A. P. Middleton, *Tobacco Coast, A Maritime History of Chesapeake Bay in the Colonial Era,* ed. George C. Mason, Newport News, 1953, p. 353; C. P. Gould, "The Economic Causes of the Rise of Baltimore," in *Essays in Colonial History Presented to Charles McLean Andrews,* New Haven, 1931, pp. 235-38.
29. H. R. Merrens, *Colonial North Carolina in the Eighteenth Century: A Study in Historical Geography,* Chapel Hill, 1964, pp. 142-72.

30. D. A. Farnie, "The Commercial Empire of the Atlantic 1607-1783," *Economic History Review*, 2nd Series, 15, 1962, pp. 205-18.

31. J. T. Lemon, "Urbanization and the Development of Eighteenth Century Southeastern Pennsylvania and Adjacent Delaware," *William and Mary Quarterly*, 3rd Series, 24, 1967, pp. 501-42.

32. G. R. Taylor, "American Urban Growth Preceding the Railway Age," *Journal of Economic History*, 27, 1967, pp. 309-39.

33. R. G. Albion, "New York Port and Its Disappointed Rivals, 1815-1860," *Journal of Economic and Business History*, 3, 1930-31, pp. 602-29.

34. J. W. Livingood, *The Philadelphia-Baltimore Trade Rivalry, 1780-1860*, Harrisburg, 1947, pp. 161-63.

35. S. E. Morison, *The Maritime History of Massachusetts, 1730-1860*, Cambridge, 1921, pp. 225-99; E. C. Kirkland, *Men, Cities and Transportation: A Study in New England History, 1820-1900*, Volume 1, Cambridge, 1948, pp. 92-93.

36. G. R. Taylor, *The Transportation Revolution*, New York, 1951, pp. 56-69; L. C. Hunter, *Steamboats on Western Rivers, American Economic and Technical History*, Cambridge, 1949, 27-32; A. F. Burghardt, "The Location of River Towns in the Central Lowland of the United States," *Annals of the Association of American Geographers*, 69, 1959, pp. 305-23.

37. A. Fishlow, *Railroads and the Transformation of the Ante Bellum Economy*, Cambridge, 1967, p. 12; G. R. Taylor, "American Economic Growth Before 1840: An Exploratory Essay," *Journal of Economic History*, 24, 1964, pp. 427-44.

38. J. G. Clark, *The Grain Trade of the Old Northwest*, Urbana, 1966, pp. 32-51, 124-171; L. C. Hunter, *op. cit.*, pp. 32-60.

39. A. Fishlow, *op. cit.*, 1967, pp. 275-88; R. W. Fogel, "American Interregional Trade in the Nineteenth Century," in R. L. Andreano, ed., *New Views in American Economic Development*, Cambridge, 1965, pp. 213-24.

40. H. H. Scheiber, "Urban Rivalry and Internal Improvement in the Old North West," *Ohio History*, 71-72, 1962-63, pp. 227-39; R. L. Ransom, "Interregional Canals and Economic Specialization in the Ante-Bellum United States," *Explorations in Entrepreneurial History*, 5, 1967, pp. 12-35; J. G. Clark, *op. cit.*, pp. 52-79.

41. R. L. Ransom, "Canals and Development: A Discussion of Issues," *Papers and Proceedings of the American Economic Association*, 54, 1964, pp. 365-76.

42. D. R. McManis, "The Initial Evaluation and Utilization of the Illinois Prairies, 1815-1840," *Department of Geography Research Paper No. 94*, Chicago, 1964.

43. A. Fishlow, *op. cit.*, pp. 18-19.

44. R. W. Fogel, "A Quantitative Approach to the Study of Railroads in American Economic Growth: A Report of Some Preliminary Findings," *Journal of Economic History*, 22, 1962, pp. 163-97; R. L. Ransom, *op. cit.*, pp. 365-77.

45. R. Higgs, *op. cit.*, pp. 369-75.

46. W. W. Belcher, *The Economic Rivalry between St. Louis and Chicago, 1850-1880*, New York, 1947, pp. 55-113; B. Still, "Patterns of Mid-Nineteenth Century Urbanization in the Middle West," *Mississippi Valley Historical Review*, 28, 1941, pp. 187-206; J. G. Clark, *op. cit.*, pp. 251-88.

47. M. Rothstein, "Ante-Bellum Wheat and Cotton Exports: A Contrast in Marketing

Organization and Economic Development," *Agricultural History*, 40, 1966, pp. 91-100.

48. M. Rothstein, "The Ante-Bellum South as a Dual Economy: A Tentative Hypothesis," *Agricultural History*, 41, 1967, pp. 373-82; S. B. Hilliard, "Pork in the Ante-Bellum South: The Geography of Self-Sufficiency," *Annals of the Association of American Geographers*, 59, 1969, pp. 461-80.

49. H. S. Perloff et al., *op. cit.*, p. 49.

50. G. C. Quiett, *They Built the West: An Epic of Rails and Cities*, New York, 1934; R. Higgs, *op. cit.*, pp. 369-75.

51. R. B. Vance and S. Smith, "Metropolitan Dominance and Integration," in R. B. Vance and N. J. Demerath, eds., *The Urban South*, Chapel Hill, 1954, pp. 114-34.

2 THE CITYWARD

MOVEMENT OF IMMIGRANTS

The exploitation of new resources and radical changes in transportation stimulated extensive selective migration among the foreign born as well as among natives of the United States. Most of these migrants left farms or small rural settlements to seek urban employment, many of the foreign-born moving directly from rural areas in Europe to American cities. Domestic migrants were frequently tempted to move West in search of new opportunities; but many moved only to a nearby city. A large proportion of the people bound for cities were foreign-born, so that by the last quarter of the nineteenth century, immigrants and their American-born children accounted for two thirds or more of the population of cities in the industrial center of the economy. In the cities of the periphery, the proportions were more varied, but in general people of foreign birth and parentage represented less than one half of the total population of each city. Whereas immigrants contributed in large part to the rapidly growing urban population of the Northeast and the Middle West, people of native parentage were most numerous among the new urban residents of western cities. Largely because the volume, timing, and destination of all migration responded to spatial changes in the national economy, American cities exhibited striking regional variations in their immigrant populations.

Most discussions of migration and urbanization have considered the cityward movement within well-defined and areally restricted limits and therefore have concentrated upon short-distance movements. Both international and inter-regional migration profoundly influenced the development of American cities, but studies of the shorter movements have revealed the relevant factors affecting urban migration. Indeed, long-distance migration often was accomplished in several stages, but frequently each successive move was to a more populous city. Consequently, most early students of urban migration agreed that there was a positive relationship between population at the destination volume of migration, and extent of the migration field.[1]

This size-distance-volume relationship has subsequently been refined by considerations of intervening opportunities, differences in income potential in alternative destinations, and the availability of information in various locations.[2] Improvements in transportation and communications made long-distance travel easier and knowledge of changes in the location of employment opportunities more readily available. These considerations were reflected in changes in both the source areas and preferred destinations of migrants.[3] A discussion of the complex motivations of individual migrants, their choice of destination, their ability to reach this goal, and their desire to move on in search of new opportunities is beyond the scope of this survey. The aggregate and cumulative result of the selective spatial mobility of millions of people was the emergence of rather striking variations in the source areas of the populations of different regions, which influenced both the volume and the composition of the movement toward cities. Although this chapter is primarily concerned with the changing regional and urban destinations of immigrants, the secular increase in the numbers of people who moved to cities—both native and foreign-born—will be explored initially.

IMMIGRATION

Between 1820 and the early 1920's, when restrictive legislation severely curtailed immigration, more than 33 million people entered the United States. Most of them settled in cities, and in 1920 fully three quarters of the foreign-born population were urban residents. Forty-eight per cent of the country's total urban population in 1920 was of foreign birth or parentage and in the cities with more than 100,000 inhabitants, which together housed about one quarter of the total population, people of foreign parentage and birth accounted for almost 58 per cent of all residents.[4] Throughout the period of mass immigration, there were more urban dwellers among people of foreign birth and parentage than among those of native parentage. During the course of the nineteenth century, the volume of immigration, like the rate of urbanization, fluctuated. The most impressive change occurred during the 1880's, when the number of immigrant arrivals increased markedly. Before 1880 less than one third of the total number of immigrants who arrived between 1820 and 1920 had entered the country. Thus, in a period of only forty years, between 1880 and 1920, an average of about six million people arrived in each decade (Table 2-1). Indeed, from 1900 through 1909, more than eight million newcomers entered.

After 1880, the source areas of immigrants shifted noticeably (Fig. 2-1). Before that time, about 85 per cent of all immigrants came from the British Isles, Germany, British America, and Scandinavia. Although people from these areas continued to arrive in large numbers for some time after 1880, they represented less than 20 per cent of the total during the decade of World War I. The number of immigrants from Italy and the Russian and Austro-Hungarian empires steadily increased and by 1896 accounted for more than half of the total immigration.

The increased scale and new sources of immigration aroused much political interest, which generated not only a major congressional investi-

TABLE 2-1

Decennial Immigration to the United States, 1820–1919

	1820 to 1829	1830 to 1839	1840 to 1849	1850 to 1859	1860 to 1869	1870 to 1879	1880 to 1889	1890 to 1899	1900 to 1909	1910 to 1919
Total in Millions	0.1	0.5	1.4	2.7	2.1	2.7	5.2	3.7	8.2	6.3
Per Cent of Total from:										
Ireland	40.2	31.7	46.0	36.9	24.4	15.4	12.8	11.0	4.2	2.6
Germany[1]	4.5	23.2	27.0	34.8	35.2	27.4	27.5	15.7	4.0	2.7
United Kingdom	19.5	13.8	15.3	13.5	14.9	21.1	15.5	8.9	5.7	5.8
Scandinavia	0.2	0.4	0.9	0.9	5.5	7.6	12.7	10.5	5.9	3.8
Canada[2]	1.8	2.2	2.4	2.2	4.9	11.8	9.4	0.1	1.5	11.2
Russia[1]					0.2	1.3	3.5	12.2	18.3	17.4
Austria-Hungary[1]					0.2	2.2	6.0	14.5	24.4	18.2
Italy					0.5	1.7	5.1	16.3	23.5	19.4

1. Continental European boundaries prior to the 1919 settlement.

2. British America to 1867; Canada includes Newfoundland; Canadian immigration was not recorded between 1886 and 1893.

From N. Carpenter, "Immigrants and Their Children," U.S. Bureau of the Census Monograph, No. 7, Washington, D.C., 1927, pp. 324-25.

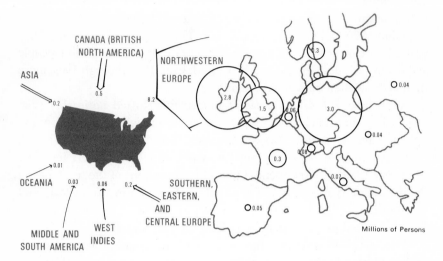

1820-1879

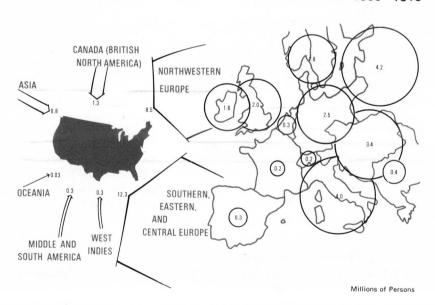

1880-1919

FIG. 2-1. Source Areas of Immigrants to the United States, 1820-1919

gation, published in 1911,[5] but also a voluminous academic and popular literature.[6] At the time, observers differed widely on the delegation of responsibilities for the social and economic problems of mass immigration, but the majority agreed that the increasing concentration of foreigners in the Northeast had reached alarming proportions. Indeed, the term "old immigrants" was frequently employed to distinguish, on the basis of both source areas and destinations, those foreigners who arrived before 1880 from the "new immigrants" who landed after that date. To some observers, this division was prejudicial and passed judgment on the relative desirability and degree of assimilation of the groups concerned. Although the majority of "old immigrants" who arrived from northwestern Europe before 1880 differed from native Americans in either language or religion, their assimilation into American society was thought to be facilitated by their widespread distribution and by their settlement on the land as well as in the cities. English-speaking immigrants alone accounted for more than half the total foreign-born population in 1880 but over one half of this proportion were Catholic Irish immigrants who were highly concentrated in the northeastern states. Among German-speaking immigrants, however, differences in religion did not exercise a strong influence upon either their distribution or assimilation.

In contrast, a larger proportion of the "new immigrants" from southern and eastern Europe were concentrated in the ghettoes of northeastern industrial cities where they scarcely encountered the society and institutions of native-born Americans. The fact that the "new immigrants" settled primarily in cities was often attributed to ignorance of opportunities elsewhere and to lack of occupational skills. Yet it was actually the demand for low-paid unskilled labor that attracted most of the "new immigrants" to industrial and commercial employment in urban centers. Although the increased volume and distant sources of the "new immigration" were related to unscrupulous promotional activities of transportation companies, most of the newcomers were joining friends and relatives already established in the New World. Also, the urban destinations of many immigrants were not determined solely by direct corporate inducements. Clearly the distinction between "new" and "old" neglected the effects of length of residence in the new country on both the distribution and assimilation of immigrants and, further, obscured major differences in the locational characteristics of individual groups.[7]

Although in 1920 the proportions of urban residents among immi-

Table 2-2

Urban Residence of Foreign-Born White Population, 1920

	Per Cent of Group Urban	Per Cent of Total Foreign-Born Urban Population
Foreign-Born White	75.5	100.0
Russia	88.6	12.0
Ireland	86.9	8.7
Italy	84.4	13.1
Poland	84.4	9.3
Hungary	80.0	2.9
United Kingdom	75.0	8.4
Austria	75.0	4.2
Canada	74.5	8.1
Yugoslavia	69.3	1.1
Germany	67.5	12.3
Czechoslovakia	66.3	2.3
Scandinavia	54.6	7.7

From N. Carpenter, "Immigrants and Their Children," *U.S. Bureau of the Census Monograph,* No. 7, Washington, D.C., 1927, p. 372.

grants from southern and eastern Europe were higher by more than 15 per cent than among those from northwestern Europe, the Irish (the second largest contributors to the "old immigration") remained one of the most highly urbanized immigrant groups throughout the entire period of mass immigration (Table 2-2). Almost 87 per cent of the people of Irish birth lived in cities, and of the major immigrant groups this proportion was exceeded only by people of Russian birth. Moreover, the contributions of several other "old immigrant" groups to the total immigrant population of all cities remained substantial in 1920 (Table 2-2). For example, 67.5 per cent of the German immigrants lived in cities, but, because of the large overall population of German birth, they accounted for more than 12 per cent of the total foreign-born population in American cities. Only Italian immigrants, of whom more than 84 per cent were urban residents, exceeded the numbers of Germans living in cities (Table 2-2). Similarly, people from the United Kingdom, Canada, and Scandinavia together accounted for more than one quarter of the total number of urban immigrants. Thus, although many ethnic and national groups of the "new immigration" settled almost exclusively in cities, only those from Russia and Italy contributed substantially more people to American cities than did most of the groups of the "old immigration."

INTERNAL MIGRATION

Although most immigrants concentrated in urban centers, their contribution relative to the total urban population was dependent on the size of the cityward movement of people born in the United States. Since the proportion of the total population resident in cities and employed in non-agricultural activities increased rather sharply in the period between the diminution of the "old" and the increase in the "new immigration," it became evident that the destinations of native-born migrants, like those of the foreign-born, became increasingly urban. To be sure, long-distance migration from older settled areas to the west accounted for much of the internal migration in the United States during the nineteenth century. Adna Weber's study of the different levels of internal migration in Europe and in the United States concludes that Americans were more accustomed to move from state to state than were Europeans from county to county.[8] Although internal migration in Britain was by far the greatest in Europe, the proportion of Americans living outside their state of birth in 1870 was slightly larger than that of Englishmen living outside their county of birth in 1871. The actual difference in internal migration was probably somewhat greater than the comparison suggests because of the difference in size between the American states and British counties. Certainly most long-distance migration in the United States was accomplished in several stages over one or more generations, as in the instance of New Englanders who had lived for several years in New York or Ohio before moving on to the far Middle West in the mid-nineteenth century.[9] Moreover, the persistence of migrant families in their initial destinations was rarely lengthy, for the turnover of residents in frontier communities was quite high.[10]

Largely because of the great publicity given to the volume of immigration and the westward movement in the nineteenth century, few observers attempted to determine the extent of the cityward movement of native Americans during the same period. Adna Weber used the Massachusetts Census of 1885 to illustrate his contention that the growth of many American cities was as much the result of the migration of native Americans as of natural increase or immigration.[11] More than 24 per cent of Boston's population in 1885 was born in the United States but outside the city limits. This proportion was only slightly lower than those recorded in large European cities at about the same time. Also, Bidwell has established that local cityward movements supported the growth of the manufacturing cities of southern New England for at least twenty years before the Irish began to immigrate in large numbers.[12] These centers attracted the majority of the local migrants even though many New Englanders had started to move westward after 1820.

For the United States as a whole, Wilcox suggests that the decline in the volume of inter-state migration after 1870 was related to an increase in local migrations to cities.[13] Between 1850 and 1870 the proportion of native-born people living outside of their state of birth increased from 23.6 to 26.2 per cent but by 1890 declined to 20.9 per cent. Although these observations for the nation as a whole simply indicate secular changes in the volume of inter-state migration, it would appear that before about 1870 opportunities in the West for urban as well as agricultural employment competed with local urban centers within the areas of emigration. Thereafter, however, the proportion of long-distance movements within the total internal migration declined, and even newly settled areas began to experience the effects of the cityward movement. Fletcher, for example, indicates that between 1880 and 1890 no less than one half of the townships in the five states of the Old Northwest recorded population losses. Yet during the same period the total population of this area increased by an average of more than 20 per cent.[14] In a more comprehensive evaluation of internal migration, Thornthwaite concludes that "the migration history of the prevailing agricultural areas followed a uniform pattern. About three decades after the first settlement, the population surplus reaches a maximum, and after about three more decades of decreasing surplus, a deficit is established."[15] Although inter-state migration diminished after 1870, large numbers of native-born residents from the North Central states moved to the rapidly urbanizing Western and Southwestern states (Fig. 2-2). Many native-born residents also left the Northeastern and Southern states, but these losses were compensated for by gains in internal migration.

The large proportion of "new immigrants" from abroad with urban destinations was probably no greater than among native-born Americans who migrated after about 1875. In some areas, a large segment of the latter were the children of immigrants who had settled on the land earlier in the century and also included many black residents of the Southern states. They moved not only to local urban centers in the South

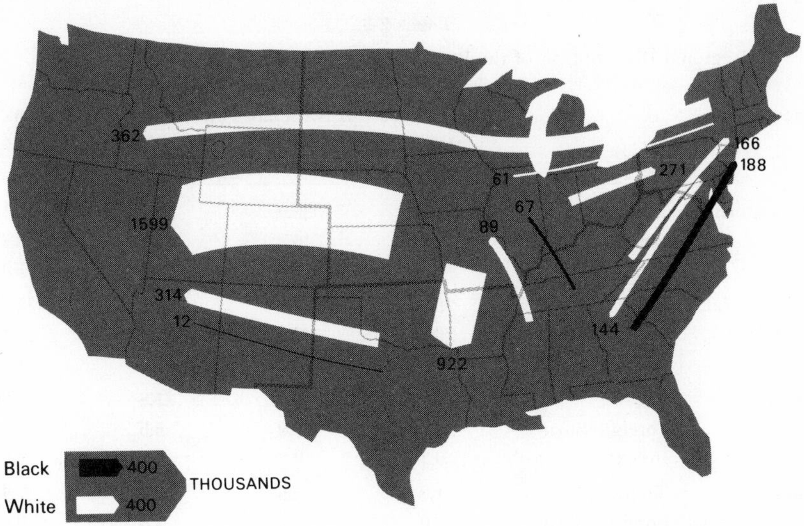

FIG. 2-2. Inter-regional Migration Within the United States, 1870-1910

(which had attracted relatively few foreigners), but also to large northern cities. Of somewhat more than 250,000 Negroes who left the South between 1870 and 1910 almost 190,000 moved to Northeastern states (Fig. 2-2). Subsequently, however, the pattern shifted and the larger numbers of black Americans went to the North Central states. But the movement of black Americans to northern cities assumed major dimensions only during and after World War I. By 1910 about one quarter of the country's Negro population lived in urban centers, and of this total almost three quarters lived in southern cities.[16] There were about 750,000 black Americans in the Northern and Western states; more than one third of whom lived in New York, Philadelphia, Chicago, and St. Louis.

THE SHIFTING LOCATION OF IMMIGRANT DESTINATIONS

Throughout the period of mass immigration, immigrants settled in the most rapidly urbanizing sections of the United States. At first many remained in their ports of arrival which (apart from New Orleans) were on the northeastern seaboard, and by 1850 almost 60 per cent of the total number of foreign-born lived in New England and the Middle Atlantic states, but already 30 per cent resided in the North Central states, the most rapidly urbanizing section of the expanding periphery. Between 1850 and 1890, however, the proportion in New England and the Middle

TABLE 2-3

Regional Distribution of the Population of the United States, 1850–1910

Region		Per Cent of National Total in a Given Region			
		1850	1870	1890	1910
Northeastern:	Total	37.2	30.9	27.7	28.1
	Foreign Born	59.0	46.9	42.6	49.7
	Index*	1.6	1.5	1.5	1.8
North Central:	Total	23.3	32.6	35.6	32.5
	Foreign Born	29.1	42.4	44.6	35.1
	Index*	1.2	1.3	1.3	1.1
Southern:	Total	38.7	30.9	31.8	32.0
	Foreign Born	10.7	7.2	5.6	5.4
	Index*	0.3	0.2	0.2	0.2
Western:	Total	1.9	6.6	4.9	7.4
	Foreign Born	1.0	4.5	7.3	9.8
	Index*	0.5	0.7	1.5	1.3

* Index = Foreign-Born Population/Total Population

Note: For boundaries see Fig. 1-2.

Atlantic states declined to 42 per cent (Table 2-3) (Fig. 2-3), as the agricultural potential of the Middle West and Northern Plains and the rapid growth of inland cities began to attract many of the new arrivals. After about 1890, the proportions in New England and the Middle Atlantic states again increased because the industrial center of the national economy was now attracting most of the immigrants. This center had expanded into the Middle West, but not enough to offset a proportionate decline in the foreign-born population of the North Central states as a whole. By 1910 almost one half of the total immigrant population lived in the Northeastern states and about one third in the North Central states. Few immigrants went to the South or the West, but whereas the proportion of foreign-born living in the South declined from 10 to 5 per cent, there was an increase in the Western states from less than 2 to almost 10 per cent (Table 2-3) (Fig. 2-4).

Some of the regional shifts in the distribution of immigrants seem, however, little different from those of the American population as a whole. In order to identify these differences, a crude deviation index has been employed, which describes the degree to which the proportion of the total foreign-born population of a given region was greater or lesser

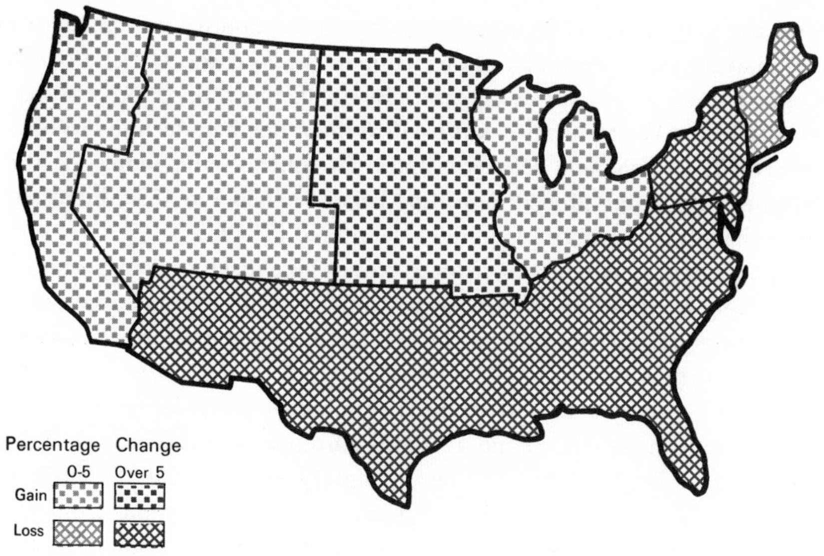

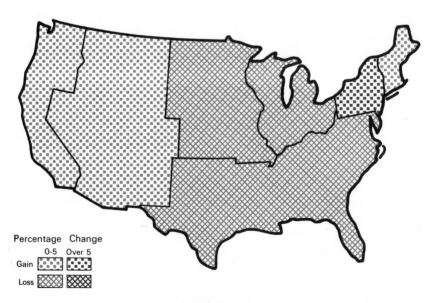

FIG. 2-3. Changes in the Regional Distribution of the Foreign-Born Population of the United States, 1850-1890

FIG. 2-4. Changes in the Regional Distribution of the Foreign-Born Population of the United States, 1890-1910

than that of the population as a whole (Table 2-3). Between 1850 and 1910 the proportion of immigrants living in the South was consistently less than the population as a whole, while in the Northeastern and North Central states it was always greater. By 1890, the proportion was also greater in the Western states, but by 1910 the index had declined in both the North Central and Western states. In contrast, the index for the Northeastern states, after diminishing between 1850 and 1890, increased quite sharply to reach a maximum value in 1910 (Table 2-3).

The increased extent and reduced cost of long-distance transportation and changing locations of new opportunities strongly influenced shifts in the regional distribution of the foreign-born population. Variations in the wealth, skills, and preferences of different immigrant groups, however, either enlarged or restricted the number of potential destinations. Even when transportation and available employment presented an identical range of destinations, different immigrant groups tended to settle in separate locations. To be sure, some areas attracted immigrants from several sources; nevertheless, shared experiences encouraged people from the same areas to stay together.

Regional Destinations Before 1850

It was the census of 1850 that first collected statistics on place of birth and recorded striking differences in the regional distribution of people of Irish and German origin. The deviation index employed earlier

TABLE 2-4

Regional Distribution of Selected Immigrant Groups, 1850

	Index of Deviation*		United Kingdom	British America	Per Cent of Foreign Born
	Ireland	Germany			
New England	1.5	0.1	0.8	2.4	13.6
Middle Atlantic	1.2	0.8	1.0	0.8	45.4
East North Central	0.5	1.6	1.2	1.1	24.6
West North Central	0.5	2.0	0.7	0.6	4.5
South	0.9	1.3	0.7	0.2	10.7
Mountain	0.5	1.0	1.5	0.5	0.2
Pacific	0.3	0.5	1.2	0.1	1.0

* Index = Foreign-Born Group/Total Foreign-Born Population

Note: For boundaries see Fig. 2-3.

has been adapted to express differences between the proportion of various immigrant groups within a given region and the immigrant population as a whole (Table 2-4). In New England and the Middle Atlantic states, the proportions of Irish-born were larger than those of the immigrant population as a whole; in the North Central and Southern states, the proportions of Germans were greater. These differences were largely the result of limitations in transatlantic transport and the ability of the German immigrants to pay for transportation inland directly upon arrival. Before about 1850, destinations of emigrants from Europe depended less upon locational preferences than on the routes and organization of transatlantic commodity commerce.[17] In the absence of specialized cheap passenger services, immigrants became the westbound ballast of Atlantic sailing ships, compensating in revenue for the difference in bulk between eastbound cargoes of raw materials and westbound cargoes of manufactured goods.

The commodity commerce between Britain and the United States was far greater than between any other European country and the New World. Certainly the vast majority of immigrants to the United States before 1850 were from the British Isles, for in that year 44 per cent of the total foreign-born population came from Ireland, 17 per cent from the rest of the British Isles, and 7 per cent from British America. Since no fewer than seventy ports in Britain had ephemeral or permanent commerce with North America, most migrants who departed before about 1830 merely went to the closest port and waited for unscheduled departures to the New World. As the volume of emigration grew larger and as internal communications in Britain improved, the immigrant traffic became increasingly concentrated in Liverpool, the major port of departure for North America.[18] New York, as the leading importer of British manufactured goods, received the largest proportion of emigrants who sailed from Liverpool.

The largest foreign-born group in the United States in 1850 was the Irish, more than one fifth of whom lived in New England. Many of them came to these states by way of British America, and Portland and Boston, which traded frequently with the Maritime Provinces, served as major ports of arrival. Indeed, British legislation discouraged direct emigration to the United States by placing more severe restrictions upon the number of passengers carried by vessels bound for the United States than on those bound for British America.[19] In 1817 rates from the British Isles to New Brunswick or Quebec were scarcely one half the rates charged to the United States. Although the cost differential decreased during the 1820's and 1830's, large numbers of Irish emigrants crossed the Atlantic on lumber ships returning from England to New Brunswick. The returning ships first carried coal and salt from English to Irish ports, then picked up emigrants and transported them directly from Ireland to North America. By the forties, English traders had engrossed the Irish lumber and flax trade and virtually all Irish commerce eventually was channeled through Liverpool. Thus, most Irish emigrants had to make a preliminary voyage eastward across the Irish sea before sailing west. The lumber ships carried passengers to New Brunswick for as little as fifteen shillings and the earnings of a season in lumber camps there would more than finance a voyage to New England or New York. Then, in 1842 with the abolition of timber duties in the British Isles, the immigrant traffic on westbound ships became more costly. Also, the development of special services for immigrants had greatly decreased the cost of passage from Liverpool direct to the northeastern American seaports.[20]

German immigrants accounted for less than 5 per cent of the total arrivals in the United States during the 1830's, but during the 1840's this proportion increased greatly, and by 1850 they represented more than a quarter of the foreign-born population. Just as Irish emigration was initially dependent upon the transatlantic lumber trade, so early emigrants from the German states and Alsace-Lorraine were reliant on tobacco ships sailing from Bremen to Baltimore, and on cotton freighters returning to New Orleans from Le Havre.[21] Although Hamburg, Rotterdam, and Antwerp also handled emigrant traffic from the continent, their role was much less because of limited commodity trade with the United States.[22] Thus Liverpool, rather than ports on the continent, competed with Bremen and Le Havre for German emigrant traffic. Arrangements were made to transport emigrants across the North Sea to Hull or Grimsby and then by rail to Liverpool. Quite apart from German immigrants who arrived by way of Liverpool, New York received an increasing proportion of German immigration as traffic became more specialized and less dependent upon existing routes of oceanic commerce.

Like the Irish immigrants, many of the Germans concentrated in their ports of arrival before 1850. Proportionately larger numbers, however, moved to the Middle West and by that date only 15 per cent of the Irish-born population, as compared with some 48 per cent of the Germans, lived in the North Central states. In general, German immigrants had greater resources than the Irish and were able to travel and purchase land more easily. For people who arrived at New Orleans, transportation to the Middle West was cheap and frequent, and immigrants who landed at Baltimore were able to take advantage of steamboat services on the Ohio River once they had crossed the Appalachians. In the Southern states, the Census of 1850 recorded many Germans who were presumably temporarily residing in New Orleans or Baltimore or in river towns on the Ohio or Misissippi. New York, of course, had excellent water routes to the interior, but before about 1850 German immigrants, like native-born Americans, remained in upstate New York or moved into the southern sections of the Middle West rather than to areas adjacent to the Great Lakes. Less than 2 per cent of the total German-born population lived in New England (which had little trade with Western Europe), while more than 20 per cent of the nation's Irish-born population resided there.

REGIONAL DESTINATIONS: 1850-1890

During the late 1840's crop failures created a Malthusian crisis in European agriculture, and emigration, particularly from Ireland, south-western Germany, and some sections of Scandinavia increased sharply. Between 1850 and 1859 no fewer than 2,750,000 immigrants arrived in the United States (Table 2-1). Although the volume of the transatlantic movements slackened in the late 1850's and during the Civil War, the pace of immigration increased rapidly in the late 1860's and reached a new peak in 1873 when more than 400,000 people arrived in one year. The depression of the mid-1870's resulted in a temporary diminution, but during the 1880's immigration reached an unprecedented volume as more than 5.3 million newcomers entered the United States (Table 2-1). Although the initial acceleration in immigration was sustained by "push" factors in Europe, improvements in both oceanic and land transportation not only increased the number of potential destinations but also reduced the time and uncertainties involved in long-distance migration.

The construction of railroads from northeastern ports to the Middle West during the 1850's and into the Great Plains and Far West after the Civil War opened large areas to commercial development. The impact of the railroad on migration was not, however, confined to technical improvements which facilitated movement. Many companies had received land grants to stimulate expansion into unsettled areas, and, consequently, they established immigration agencies to advertise the potential of these holdings.[23] Indeed, companies often discounted all or part of the expense of transportation from the cost of land purchased by immigrants while through-tickets and group rates were provided from remote parts of Europe to newly settled sections of the country. Several of the states also established similar agencies to promote rapid settlement, and, certainly, the information available in Europe about opportunities in the New World encouraged many immigrants to move directly from their original homes to newly opened regions of the United States.

Improvements in ocean transport also facilitated long-distance migration. Sailing ships, often American-owned, moved most of the immigrants before the Civil War, but during the 1860's British steamships established a preeminence in Atlantic crossings, reducing the time involved from between one and three months to about ten days.[24] The steamships also encouraged a greater concentration of the immigrant traffic in Liverpool and New York, but with the entry of German competition Bremen retained its position as the leading emigrant port on the European mainland. Both German and British steamship companies pioneered new ports of emigration in Europe, and, as the flow from southern and eastern Europe increased, New York continued to receive an overwhelming proportion of the immigrants.

The improved accessibility and knowledge of conditions and opportunities in the interior of the country increased the proportion of immigrants who moved directly inland from their ports of arrival (Fig. 2-3). Most of them settled in the North Central states, where by 1890 more immigrants resided than on the northeastern seaboard (Table 2-3). The proportion of foreign-born people in the Far Western states also increased rapidly but amounted to only 7 per cent of the total in 1880. Very few of the immigrants moving inland went to the South, and between 1850 and 1890 the proportion of the nation's foreign-born people living there was halved to only 5 per cent. This change in distribution resulted primarily from the settlement of large numbers of Germans and Scandinavians in the cities and newly established farms of the North Central states.[25] By 1850, there were many German immigrants in the Middle West, and during the following four decades, when the German States provided by far the largest source of immigrants, the North Central states continued to attract proportionately more German-born people than foreign-born people as a whole (Table 2-5). Germans also remained well represented in the small immigrant group in the South, and between 1870 and 1890 the proportion of their total numbers in the Middle At-

TABLE 2-5

Regional Distribution of Selected Immigrant Groups, 1870

Index of Deviation*

	Ireland	Germany	United Kingdom	Canada	Scandi-navia	Per Cent of Foreign Born
New England	1.6	0.1	0.9	2.7	0.1	11.8
Middle Atlantic	1.4	0.9	1.1	0.6	0.2	34.1
East North Central	0.6	1.4	1.0	1.1	1.4	30.2
West North Central	0.6	1.2	0.7	0.9	3.6	12.2
South	0.9	1.3	0.7	0.2	0.3	7.2
Mountain	0.4	0.3	2.6	0.9	2.6	1.4
Pacific	1.0	0.6	1.1	0.8	0.7	3.1

* Index = Foreign-Born Group/Total Foreign-Born Population

Note: For boundaries see Fig. 2-3.

lantic states increased to equal the proportion of the total immigrant population in that section. There were larger proportions of Scandinavians than the foreign-born population as a whole only in the North Central states, but in the western parts of those states the proportion was almost three times larger than the whole immigrant population (Table 2-5).

Although agricultural opportunities in the interior attracted increasingly large numbers of immigrants, the Irish continued to prefer New England and the Middle Atlantic states to the North Central states, where the proportion of the nation's Irish-born was only one half that of the total foreign-born population (Table 2-5). Although Canadian immigrants were proportionately well represented in the East North Central states, New England was their leading destination.[26] Canadians who settled there came largely from French-speaking areas; nevertheless, Boston and its vicinity attracted considerable numbers of Maritimers and Newfoundlanders. The Canadians in the East North Central states presumably moved from Ontario into adjacent sections of the United States, although French-speaking Canadians also moved to the west. Differences in the destinations of the Irish, Germans, Canadians, and Scandinavians, were clearly established between 1850 and 1890 and endured through the following twenty years, when the sources and volume of immigration changed quite rapidly.

Downtown at the Mid-Nineteenth Century

Chicago's Warehouse District, South Water Street, *c.* 1870
Courtesy Chicago Historical Society

New York's Warehouse District, Liberty Street near Broadway, 1836-37
The Edward W. C. Arnold Collection, Museum of the City of New York

Chicago's Financial Nucleus, La Salle and Lake Streets, 1856
Courtesy Chicago Historical Society

New York's Financial Nucleus, Wall Street, 1834
The Edward W. C. Arnold Collection, Museum of the City of New York

REGIONAL DESTINATIONS: 1890-1910

During the 1880's, German, British, Canadian, and Scandinavian immigrants to the United States were the most numerous, but, during the same decade, almost 750,000 people came from Italy and the Russian and Austro-Hungarian empires (Table 2-1). Then, during the 1890's, when the total volume of immigration had declined, the number of arrivals from southern and eastern Europe more than doubled. From 1900 to 1909 more than 6 million immigrants from Italy and the two eastern European empires arrived in the United States, resulting in an unprecedented total immigration for those years: more than eight million people (Table 2-1).

These shifts in the source areas of immigrants partially resulted from influences far removed from the potentialities of more remunerative employment in the United States.[27] For example, because of industrial developments in Germany and Sweden, many potential emigrants were intercepted or retained, and Canada and Australia became more competitive alternatives to emigrants from the British Isles. In addition, political persecution accelerated the emigration of Jews from the Russian Empire, while the removal of restraints upon free movement stimulated emigration from the Slavic areas of the Austro-Hungarian Empire. Finally, improved internal communications in Europe and extended steamship service greatly enlarged the migration field of the United States.

The changing labor needs of the American economy were, nevertheless, compelling influences in emphasizing the new sources of migrant flows.[28] The comparative advantages of unskilled employment in daylaboring or heavy industry were far greater to the peasants and small townsmen of eastern Europe and southern Italy than they were to residents of the more industrialized and urbanized sections of northwestern Europe. Certainly, the fluctuations in the number of immigrants arriving annually in the United States were closely synchronized with changes in the business cycle after 1870 which suggests that the labor demands of the American economy strongly influenced the volume of immigration.[29]

The labor needs of the American economy also affected the immigrants' choice of destinations. Until about 1840, the greatest demands for unskilled labor were from the industrial center of the northeast; eventually, the North Central states attracted the leading proportion of immigrants. Although in 1890 most of the Irish immigrants lived in the

TABLE 2-6

Regional Distribution of Selected Immigrant Groups, 1890

Index of Deviation*

	Ireland	Germany	United Kingdom	Canada	Scandinavia	Russia	Italy	Austria-Hungary	Per Cent of Foreign Born
New England	1.8	0.2	1.1	3.1	0.4	0.5	0.7	0.1	12.6
Middle Atlantic	1.5	1.0	1.2	0.4	0.3	1.5	1.9	1.3	30.0
East North Central	0.6	1.4	0.8	1.0	1.1	0.6	0.3	1.0	27.4
West North Central	0.5	1.1	0.7	0.8	2.7	1.4	0.2	1.3	17.0
South	0.9	1.3	0.9	0.3	0.2	0.8	1.7	1.2	5.6
Mountain	0.6	0.4	2.2	1.0	1.7	0.7	1.5	0.7	2.7
Pacific	0.9	0.7	1.2	1.1	1.2	0.9	2.1	0.5	4.6

* Index = Foreign-Born Group/Total Foreign-Born Population

Note: For boundaries see Fig. 2-4.

Middle Atlantic states and New England, the increased accessibility and potential of newly settled sections of the West had attracted the majority of all newcomers. To be sure, many immigrants who went to the North Central states settled in urban centers. Between 1850 and 1890, however, the expanding industrial center of the American economy had continued to attract large numbers of immigrants to New England and the Middle Atlantic states but, after 1890, employment opportunities in the industrial center multiplied rapidly and agricultural settlement in the periphery had passed its peak. Consequently, between 1890 and 1910, the proportion of total foreign-born population in the Middle Atlantic states increased (Fig. 2-4). Although the industrial sources of employment attracted large numbers of immigrants to the East North Central states, the impressive growth of the immigrant population in the Middle Atlantic states resulted in a proportionate decline in the Middle West as a whole.

The destinations chosen by immigrants from southern and eastern Europe differed less than those of the Germans and Irish.[30] For example, most of the immigrants from Italy and the Russian Empire settled in the Middle Atlantic states, and, although limited numbers of Italians lived in the coastal cities of New England and the Southern and Pacific states (Table 2-6), by 1910 only the Middle Atlantic states had substantially greater proportions of the total Italian-born population than of the immigrant population as a whole (Table 2-7). Russian immigrants settled in the West North Central states as well as the Middle Atlantic region, and by 1890 the Russian-born proportions in both areas were greater than those of their total foreign-born populations. The majority of those in the West North Central states were Mennonites or other German-speaking people from the Ukraine; most of the people in the Middle Atlantic states were Jews from the Pale. Between 1890 and 1910 the Jewish proportion of the total immigration from the Russian Empire increased to more than 90 per cent, and accordingly, by 1910 only in the Middle Atlantic states was the proportion of Russian immigrants larger than the foreign-born population as a whole (Table 2-7). Of all the new immigrant groups, only people from the Austro-Hungarian Empire moved inland from the Middle Atlantic region in large numbers. Many people from the Hapsburg Empire who were born in the areas that later became Austria and Czechoslovakia, moved inland to all sections of the North Central states while people from the territories that became Poland, Hungary, and Yugoslavia settled almost entirely in the East North Central

TABLE 2-7
Regional Distribution of Selected Immigrant Groups, 1910

	Index of Deviation*								Per Cent of Foreign Born
	Ireland	Germany	United Kingdom	Canada	Scandinavia	Russia	Italy	Austria-Hungary	
New England	1.8	0.2	1.3	3.2	0.5	0.9	1.0	0.4	13.6
Middle Atlantic	1.3	0.8	1.0	0.3	0.3	1.5	1.6	1.4	36.1
East North Central	0.6	1.6	0.8	1.0	1.1	0.8	0.5	1.3	23.0
West North Central	0.5	1.4	0.7	0.7	3.2	0.6	0.2	0.7	12.1
South	0.7	1.4	0.9	0.3	0.3	0.8	1.1	0.7	5.4
Mountain	0.6	0.5	1.9	0.9	1.6	0.4	0.8	0.7	3.3
Pacific	0.8	0.8	1.3	1.2	1.7	0.3	0.9	0.4	6.5

* Index = Foreign-Born Group/Total Foreign-Born Population

Note: For boundaries see Fig. 2-4.

states where they tended to concentrate in areas devoted primarily to heavy industrial production. Thus, by 1910, former residents of the Austro-Hungarian Empire were present in the East North Central states in larger proportions than either Italian or Russian-Jewish immigrants who had tended to seek the more diversified employment opportunities of the metropolitan centers of the northeastern seaboard (Tables 2-6 and 2-7). Indeed, after 1890, when most newly arrived immigrants concentrated in the expanding industrial center of the American economy, variations in employment opportunities amongst the cities of this highly urbanized region influenced the destinations of different foreign-born groups and the discussion will now examine more specifically the urban destinations of immigrants.

THE URBAN DESTINATIONS OF IMMIGRANTS

Most immigrants either made their original destination a city or moved to an urban center soon after settling in a rural area, and the particular choices of different groups contributed significantly to the striking variations in the sizes and compositions of the foreign-born populations of American cities. Although populous cities attracted the largest absolute numbers, the proportionate size of the foreign-born population of a city was not closely related to the size of its total population. Large cities in the Northeast and Middle West had proportionately high numbers of foreign-born people, but in the cities of the South and West the reverse was true. Moreover, in 1870 when an average of 34 per cent of the people in the fifty most populous cities were of foreign birth, five of the fourteen cities with more than 100,000 people (Philadelphia, New Orleans, Louisville, Baltimore, and Washington, D. C.) contained less than the average proportion of immigrants (Fig. 2-5). Indeed, fewer than one quarter of the residents of Baltimore and Washington were foreign-born. By 1910 there were forty-nine cities with more than 100,000 people, but an average of only 29 per cent of their total population were immigrants, and of the nineteen centers with more than 250,000 people, only in eight was the average proportion of foreign-born exceeded (Fig. 2-6).

Cities with the largest proportion of immigrants possessed one or more of three attractive or retentive characteristics. First, ports of arrival not only retained immigrants who were destitute and unable to travel inland, but also presented opportunities to people who originally intended to settle in the interior. Second, because after 1840 immigrants

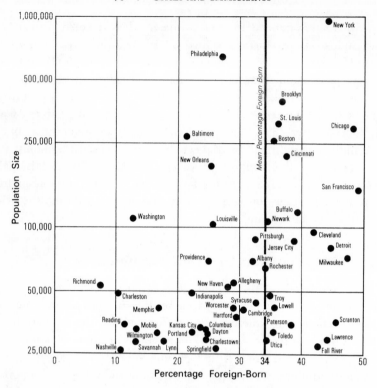

FIG. 2-5. Population Size and Foreign-Born Proportions of Large American Cities, 1870

were well represented in the movement to the North Central states, from the time of initial settlement proportionately large numbers of them lived there in the supply and export centers. Third, specialized manufacturing or mining centers which demanded unusually large amounts of cheap and unskilled labor attracted many immigrants. Although this type of employment generally supported moderate rather than large populations, similar developments also occurred within or adjacent to heavily populated cities.

Before the Civil War immigrants entered the United States through many ports, but during the 1860's New York attracted an overwhelming proportion of the immigrant flow, particularly traffic destined for the Middle Atlantic and North Central states. Although the majority of immigrants moving to the hinterlands of Boston and San Francisco continued to land in those ports, by 1870 both immigrant traffic and the proportions of foreign-born in other major ports, such as Philadelphia,

Baltimore, and New Orleans had declined. In contrast, settlements adjacent to Manhattan, such as Brooklyn, Jersey City, and Newark, attracted many immigrants who found it necessary or rewarding to settle near their port of arrival. By 1870 more than 35 per cent of the populations of all the major cities in the Ohio-Mississippi Valley and Great Lakes area (with the exception of Louisville) were of foreign birth (Fig. 2-5). All the remaining settlements with relatively large foreign-born populations were specialized manufacturing towns in New England or the Middle Atlantic states.

Although the number of cities with proportionately large numbers of immigrants increased quite rapidly between 1870 and 1910, the dominant destinations remained unchanged. The New York area, Boston, and San Francisco continued to attract large immigrant populations—in New York numerically as well as proportionately (Fig. 2-6). In Philadelphia,

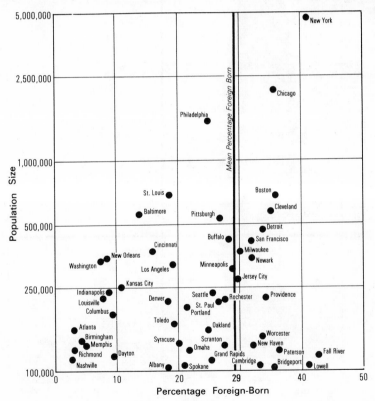

FIG. 2-6. Population Size and Foreign-Born Proportions of Large American Cities, 1910

Baltimore, and New Orleans, however, the proportions were lower than they had been in 1870. During the same period the number of specialized industrial towns with large proportions of immigrants increased greatly, particularly in New England and Middle Atlantic regions. Only the Great Lakes cities in the North Central states maintained proportionately large immigrant populations. Whereas foreign-born proportions in Cincinnati and St. Louis declined between 1870 and 1910, those of Chicago, Cleveland, Detroit, and Milwaukee either increased or remained at a level well above the average for the nation's cities as a whole (Fig. 2-6).

Because regional concentrations of the leading immigrant groups

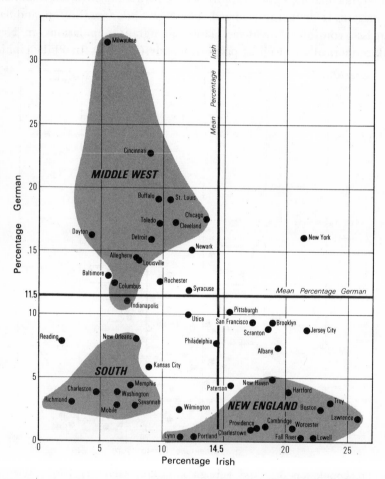

FIG. 2-7. Irish and German-Born Proportions of Large American Cities, 1870

varied, there were differences not only in the relative sizes of the foreign-born populations of cities but also in the relative proportions of different immigrant groups. By 1870, for example, Irish-born immigrants accounted for 14.3 per cent of the total population of the fifty largest cities in the nation and German-born for 11.5 per cent. The proportions of Germans in the Middle West and upstate New York were considerably higher than average, while the proportions of Irish were somewhat lower. Newark and Baltimore were the only east coast cities in this German category (Fig. 2-7); almost all the cities in the Middle Atlantic states had fewer Germans and more Irishmen than the average for the fifty largest cities as a whole. In the cities of New England (where Canadians instead of Germans were the second largest group of immigrants) the proportions of Irish-born were even higher than in the Middle Atlantic cities, while representations of both groups were lower than average in the South (Fig. 2-7).

By 1910 the proportions of both Germans and Irishmen living in cities had declined. This was partly because immigration from these sources had decreased and partly because people from southern and eastern Europe tended to concentrate in the northeastern cities. Although in 1910 only 5.4 per cent of the total populations of cities with more than 100,000 people were of Irish birth, and only 3.6 per cent of German birth, variations in the relative proportions of the two groups in different cities had hardly changed (Fig. 2-8). Because the majority of western cities with more than 100,000 people had attained their high rank during the time when most of the newly arrived people were destined for the cities of the Northeast (but after the period of the greatest influx of Irish and Germans), lower than average proportions of these groups were the rule in most western and southern cities (Fig. 2-8).

Although immigrants from Italy and the Russian and Austro-Hungarian empires concentrated in the Middle Atlantic states, their choice of destinations differed. Generally the Italians and Russian Jews settled in metropolitan cities with diversified employment opportunities. The commercial centers of the Middle Atlantic coast, in particular, housed well over half of the total number of Jewish immigrants in the United States. The highest proportions of Italians usually were found in the commercial centers of the northeastern coast. Several of the smaller ports of New England also housed large proportions of Italians but only modest proportions of Jews (Fig. 2-9). The majority of immigrants from the Austro-Hungarian Empire were from Poland, Czechoslovakia, and Hungary, and

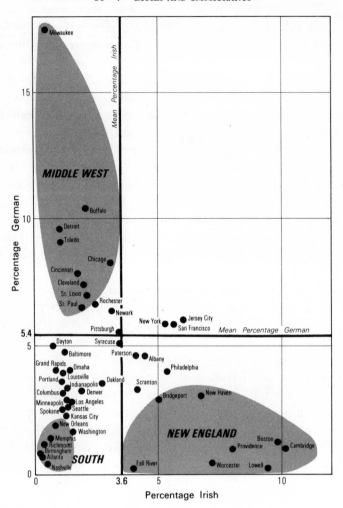

FIG. 2-8. Irish and German-Born Proportions of Large American Cities, 1910

many of these Slavic and Magyar speakers lived in New York and Newark as well as in industrial cities in the interior, such as Cleveland, Chicago, Detroit, Milwaukee, and Pittsburgh. The proportions of Italian and Russian immigrants in these cities were below average but Russians were often present in large numbers (Fig. 2-9).

(To sum up, during the course of mass immigration between 1840 and the outbreak of World War I, increasingly large shares of the foreign-born as well as migrants of native birth moved to urban centers. Improvements in ocean and land transportation and the greater availability of information directed immigrants to areas of rapid economic growth, but the timing of arrival and the limitations or potential for employment resulted in variations in the choice of destinations for different groups. Clearly distributional patterns overlapped, since the majority of all immigrant groups was heavily concentrated in New England and the Middle Atlantic and East North Central States. Nevertheless, variations in both the size and ethnic compositions of American cities were dependent on the retentive characteristics of ports of arrival and the changing location and specializations of interior centers of economic growth.)

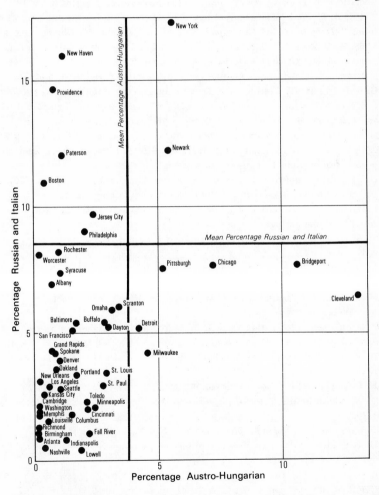

FIG. 2-9. Austro-Hungarian and Combined Russian and Italian-Born Proportions of Large American Cities, 1910

NOTES

1. E. G. Ravenstein, "The Laws of Migration," *Journal of the Royal Statistical Society*, 52, 1889, pp. 241-301; A. F. Weber, *The Growth of Cities in the Nineteenth Century*, New York, 1899, p. 259.
2. A. Stouffer, "Intervening Opportunities: A Theory Relating to Mobility and Distance," *American Sociological Review*, 5, 1940, p. 846; T. Hagerstrand, "Migration and Area, Survey of a Sample of Swedish Migration Fields and Hypothetical Considerations of Their Genesis," *Lund Studies in Geography*, Series B, 13, 1957, pp. 27-154; A. R. Pred, "The External Relations of Cities During the Industrial Revolution," *Department of Geography Research Paper No. 76*, Chicago, 1962, pp. 57-68; R. L. Morrill, "Migration and the Spread and Growth of Urban Settlement," *Lund Studies in Geography*, Series B, 26, 1965, pp. 42-48.
3. S. Kuznets, "Introduction: Population Redistribution, Migration, and Economic Growth," in H. T. Eldridge and D. S. Thomas, eds., *Population Redistribution and Economic Growth, United States, 1870-1950*, Volume 3, *Demographic Analyses and Interrelations*, Philadelphia, 1964, pp. xxiii-xxxv.
4. N. Carpenter, "Immigrants and Their Children," *U.S. Bureau of the Census Monograph*, No. 7, Washington, D.C., 1927, pp. 310-15. (Foreign parentage includes people with only one foreign-born parent.)
5. U.S. Senate Document, No. 338, 61st Congress, 2nd Session, Serial No. 5665, *Report of the Immigration (Dillingham) Commission*, Washington, D.C., 1911.
6. Library of Congress, *Immigration into the United States: A Selected List of References*, Washington, 1943.
7. M. A. Jones, *American Immigration*, Chicago, 1962, pp. 177-206.
8. A. F. Weber, *op. cit.*, p. 250.
9. L. D. Stilwell, "Migration from Vermont: 1776-1860," *Proceedings of the Vermont Historical Society*, 5, 1937, pp. 63-246.
10. M. L. Curti, *The Making of an American Community*, Stanford, 1959.
11. A. F. Weber, *op. cit.*, p. 265.
12. P. W. Bidwell, "Population Growth in Southern New England, 1810-1860," *Publications of the American Statistical Association*, New Series, 15, 1916-17, pp. 813-39.
13. W. F. Wilcox, "Decrease of Interstate Migration," *Political Science Quarterly*, 10, 1895, pp. 604-5.
14. H. J. Fletcher, "The Doom of the Small Town," *Forum*, 19, 1895, pp. 214-23.
15. C. W. Thornthwaite, *Internal Migration in the United States*, Philadelphia, 1934, p. 10.
16. T. J. Woofter, Jr., *Negro Problems in Cities*, New York, 1928, pp. 26-36.
17. M. L. Hansen, "The Second Colonization of New England," *New England Quarterly*, 2, 1929, pp. 539-60.
18. E. C. Guillet, *The Great Migration: The Atlantic Crossing by Sailing Ship Since 1770*, Toronto, 1963, pp. 47-52; M. A. Jones, *op. cit.*, pp. 104-6.
19. W. F. Adams, *Ireland and the Irish Immigration to the New World from 1815 to the Famine*, New Haven, 1932, pp. 96-97.

20. *Ibid.,* pp. 403-5.

21. M. L. Hansen, *op. cit.,* pp. 539-60.

22. T. W. Page, "The Transportation of Immigrants and Reception Arrangements in the Nineteenth Century," *Journal of Political Economy,* 19, 1911, pp. 732-49.

23. Paul W. Gates, *The Illinois Central Railroad and Its Colonization Work,* Cambridge, 1936; R. C. Overton, *Burlington West: A Colonization History of the Burlington West,* Cambridge, 1941.

24. M. A. Jones, *op. cit.,* pp. 184-85.

25. A. B. Faust, *The German Element in the United States,* Boston and New York, 1909; J. A. Hawgood, *The Tragedy of German-America,* New York, 1940; F. E. Janson, *The Background of Swedish Immigration, 1840-1930,* Philadelphia, 1931.

26. M. L. Hansen, *The Mingling of the Canadian and American Peoples,* New Haven, 1940.

27. P. Roberts, *The New Immigration: A Study of the Industrial and Social Life of Southeast Europeans in America,* New York, 1913; S. Joseph, *Jewish Immigration to the United States from 1881 to 1910,* New York, 1914; R. F. Foerster, *The Italian Emigration of Our Times,* Cambridge, 1919.

28. I. A. Hourwich, *Immigration and Labor: The Economic Aspects of European Immigration to the United States,* New York, 1912, pp. 61-102.

29. B. Thomas, *Migration and Economic Growth: A Study of Great Britain and the Atlantic Economy,* Cambridge, 1954, pp. 83-96.

30. F. J. Warne, *The Tide of Immigration,* New York, 1916, pp. 220-25.

3 THE EXPANSION AND

DIFFERENTIATION OF URBAN EMPLOYMENT

Both regional variations in the rate of urbanization and changes in the migrants' choice of destinations have been related to areal expansion and regional differentiation in the national economy. Although the volume and source of the cityward movement varied from region to region and from city to city, the sources of urban employment tended to occupy similar locations. Whereas the two previous chapters have endeavored to specify the changing and diverse urban consequences of economic development and migration in different sections of the country, this chapter and the two following ones, which treat urban employment and residence, emphasize changes in the internal spatial arrangements of people and activities common to most American cities.

Very few historical investigations of American cities have been directly concerned with the ecological implications of their rapid growth, and while the generic features of their present internal spatial structure have attracted considerable attention, the changing intra-urban locations of activities have been traced in only a few cities. Thus, the purpose of the following discussion is to emphasize the concentration of long established and newly developed employment opportunities in emerging central business districts and in the adjacent and interspersed areas devoted to manufacturing. Needless to say, the amount, type, and range of employment varied from city to city, but during the second half of the nineteenth century, it tended to concentrate in central locations in almost all American cities.

Although the Industrial Revolution is associated with the increased scale and mechanization of commodity production, employment opportunities expanded rapidly in the commercial and service activities. Indeed, handicraft manufacturing had employed most of the urban labor force long before the Industrial Revolution, but the producer himself generally arranged for the sale of his goods or services within an extremely circumscribed area. The newly mechanized and reorganized manufacturing industries continued to attract most of the labor force during the nineteenth century, yet several factors—including the differentiation of production and distribution, the rapid enlargement of market areas, and an increase in per capita wealth—multiplied employment opportunities in trade, transportation, services, and the professions. Moreover, newly established private and public utilities and services accelerated the growth of not only tertiary activities but also of general laboring and the construction industry.

Some of the opportunities for employment were widely dispersed throughout the city and others were dependent on specialized site characteristics, but by far the largest expansion of urban employment occurred in central locations. Because it was long assumed that costs were reduced through maximum accessibility to local markets, it was also assumed that the activities occupying the most central sites were those that derived the greatest advantage from savings in transportation costs.[1] The spatial ordering of land use, therefore, was determined by the varying degrees to which different businesses were able to profit from the use of expensive central space, but, because locations on the major arteries of a city are more accessible to local markets than sites in intervening areas at the same distance from the city center, the outward expansion from the original cluster of centrally located activities tended to be spoke-like.[2]

The spatial implications of this relationship were influenced by several other factors. For example, in the competition for a given location the user with the smallest areal requirements was in a position to bid a higher unit-area price for land.[3] Similarly, businesses which served particular segments of the local market did not necessarily derive advantages from a central location, and the cost of intra-urban transportation frequently represented only a small fragment of the expenses of businesses serving a national rather than a local market.[4] Furthermore, over the years, the diseconomies of congestion and problems of structural obsolescence in central areas severely diminished the advantages of superior access to the rest of the city. However, the high initial costs of land and buildings and the legal complexities of ownership have tended to delay or restrict adjustments to changes in local accessibility.[5] The inertia of central land use was also rooted in local "agglomeration" or "external" economies that were particularly vital to businesses with an irregular demand for a variable product or service. Within central locations such economies resulted from the availability of immediate and frequent information on fluctuating market conditions or individual customer needs, and of financial, technical, and distributional facilities which individual firms were unable to support.[6]

For the past fifty years, in spite of the high costs and legal difficulties of relocation and the compensations of agglomeration economies, the expansion of urban markets and the improvements in transportation and communication have encouraged many established businesses to decentralize and most new enterprises to adopt suburban sites. Previously, however, many urban activities depended on agglomeration economies, and the compact dimensions of the urban market and the high costs of horse and wagon transport discouraged decentralization.[7] Although terminal transfers were rarely convenient or efficient, railroad and waterfront facilities in central locations attracted many businesses dependent on non-local supplies or markets that could profit from minimal intra-urban movements. Consequently, at a time when the streetcar made it possible for part of the labor force to live in the suburbs, most sources of employment remained in central locations. To be sure, many businesses with noxious characteristics, such as slaughterhouses, or heavy industrial developments with expensive site requirements were established on the fringe of the built-up area, but their initial advantages eventually were obliterated by the physical expansion of the city. Some of these businesses relocated beyond the city limits, but others eventually coalesced with the expanding edge of the central business and industrial quarters.

The tendency of urban employment to concentrate in central areas was accompanied by a process of internal spatial differentiation and selective outward expansion.[8] Although the timing and scale of this process varied according to the age and functional complexity of each city, it is possible to identify the changes common to most American cities through a hypothetical example (Fig. 3-1). Until the mid-nineteenth century, apart from the small exclusive residential quarters of the rich, the functional specialization of urban land uses was only weakly developed. Most industrial and commercial activities generally were conducted on the premises of the producer or merchant, and local purchases or services were obtained on a custom basis directly from the producer. In large

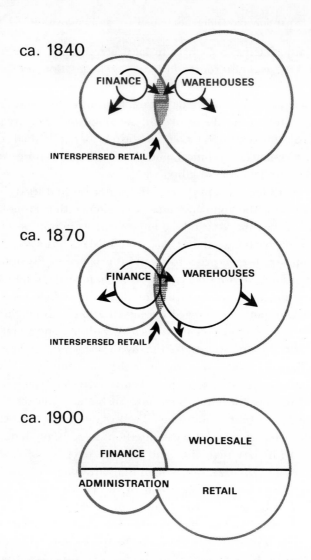

ca. 1840

FINANCE   WAREHOUSES

INTERSPERSED RETAIL

ca. 1870

FINANCE   WAREHOUSES

INTERSPERSED RETAIL

ca. 1900

FINANCE   WHOLESALE

ADMINISTRATION   RETAIL

FIG. 3-1. Generalized Stages in the Emergence of the Central Business District, 1840-1900

cities, quite small areas were devoted to the market halls which sold produce from the immediate hinterland, to the waterfront warehouses that handled exotic staples, and to the exclusive retail trade of the affluent. Between 1840 and 1870, an extensive warehouse district devoted to both manufacturing and commerce emerged as the dominant central urban land use, and, although the financial area was often well defined, it was very small. During the three decades that followed, the warehouse quarter continued to house wholesale trade and manufacturing industries, but financial and administrative districts were greatly enlarged and extensive new districts were developed to handle retail trade. Thus, central districts experienced two distinct periods of growth, one before 1870 involving minimal internal differentiation of activities and a second after 1870 in which concentration was accompanied by the spatial separation of the increasing number of centrally located activities. However, it must be stressed that this chronological definition of these two phases of growth is extremely generalized and striking variations may result not only from differences in the age, size, and hierarchical position of individual cities but also from the method and criteria used to identify specialized land uses.

THE EMERGENCE AND EXPANSION OF THE WAREHOUSE DISTRICTS

During the first of these two periods, warehouse districts expanded rapidly and temporarily dominated central land use in both long settled and newly established cities. Warehouses were not only storage areas but also served as the factories which eventually provided most of the employment for the rapidly mechanizing manufacturing sector. In most inland cities the emergence of the warehouse district was coincident with early growth, and most of the new accommodation was devoted to commercial activities. Yet in the northeastern seaports warehouses had for long lined the wharves and had expanded considerably only after 1840, when the need to accommodate newly mechanized handicraft industries arose. Throughout the colonial period, coastal and oceanic commerce had supported employment in the processing and redistribution of exotic commodities as well as in the servicing, maintenance, and provisioning of ships.[9] With the rapid expansion of international and especially transatlantic commerce after the Napoleonic Wars, warehouse and wharf construction in the major northeastern seaports not only extended specialized waterfront land uses but also encouraged the specialization, by place and commodity, of different sections of the waterfront.[10] In order to serve the complex financial requirements of long-distance trade, small but distinctive clusters of banks and insurance companies also developed near the warehouses—often in residence-counting houses recently abandoned by merchants who had built new houses well separated from the congestion and disorder of the waterfront.

The material needs of the mercantile labor force and the maintenance of vessels created a local market for cheaply made clothing, footwear, and hardware. The market gradually enlarged as these items were included in export cargoes,[11] but the response to increased demand did not result in the concentration of new manufacturing close to the waterfront. Instead, much of the gain in aggregate production resulted from the "putting-out" system. Handicraft production usually served the needs of a few rich customers; the material belongings of most urban residents either were secondhand or crudely produced by the people themselves. Once merchants became aware of the market potential of cheaply made goods, they encouraged local craftsmen to break the production process into stages and to "put-out" the work requiring unskilled labor to nearby homes or rural settlements. Thus, the craftsman was left free to concentrate on the skilled operations.[12] In this system, the merchant functioned as the central organizing agent, assuming risks, discovering markets, and providing raw materials (which he owned throughout the manufacturing process). Because production was almost entirely by hand and marketing was neither orderly nor systematic, there were as yet no advantages to be derived from concentration.

The rapid settlement of the western interior and effective inter-regional railroad systems created a new market potential for many of the craft industries. There was a quick response to the enlarged market, made possible by many small but intricate mechanical innovations which greatly reduced the skilled labor inputs in several industries. Innovations like the lathe did not entirely eliminate the "putting-out" system or the skilled craftsman, but they did reduce the proportionate shares of both in the total production sequence and encouraged a more clustered arrangement of the different stages. Merchants or master craftsmen with enough funds and knowledge to enter the marketing field organized production from central workshops where the skilled work was performed and the final product assembled. Unskilled tasks were put out to sub-contractors who utilized female labor in residential quarters or occasionally male labor in cramped workshops, yet the precise organization of the process varied from industry to industry and also from place to place. For example, in the footwear and cabinet-making industries, the central shop engrossed a large segment of the production in order to facilitate supervision of semiskilled operations.[13] Indeed, the furniture industry tended to subcontract for special operations such as upholstering and french polishing rather than for unskilled work. In contrast, in the clothing industry of most cities, sewing machines were generally leased out by merchants, resulting in increased household production. Boston was an exception, however; there, local merchants preferred to install their machines in workshops employing as many as a hundred workers.[14]

In spite of these variations, the dominant role of the merchant or jobber in distributing manufactured goods and in organizing subcontracts attracted most of the new workshops to the warehouse district. Similarly, in a pedestrian city, quick response to the elastic and unpredictable market for many products was dependent on proximity to the merchants' central shop and warehouse. Warehouses also provided rent economies, for their attics and back rooms, which were of little use for storage or display, provided adequate space for the compact machinery of a workshop. Because individual merchants utilized the services of many different subcontractors and each subcontractor relied on the orders of several merchants, the vertically disintegrated production sequence became increasingly dependent upon the "agglomeration" and "external" economies created by "clustering" in the warehouse district. Although the financial section did not expand outward on the same scale as the warehouse sections, the two central land uses generally remained adjacent and functionally related, for the merchants not only obtained credit and insurance from the financial section but also much of their market information. These developments were most characteristic of the northeastern ports, for inland cities initially relied on the older coastal cities for many of their manufactured goods. However, because of the increasing number of jobbers who extended credit to retailers and arranged for the large-scale transfer of manufactured goods, inland storage facilities were eventually built.[15]

The warehouse-workshop units of production represented a substantial advance in the scale of manufacturing, but the number of employees in each establishment rarely exceeded fifty, and the average was generally between fifteen and twenty-five. Clearly the warehouse quarter was less suitable for industries that had been able to consolidate the entire production process within a single plant, and economies of scale rather than the advantages of adjacent facilities dictated their locational pattern. For example, agricultural processing and the foundry and textile industries sought spacious waterside sites, often on the edge of the built-up area of a city or completely removed from existing large settlements.[16] The subsequent growth of many cities later absorbed and surrounded these formerly peripheral or isolated locations, many of which were scarcely one or two miles from the city center.

Although the construction of railroad systems was primarily responsible for the enlarged market of the merchant and manufacturer, the influence of the new urban terminal facilities on the location and growth of urban manufacturing was neither direct nor simple.[17] In Middle Western and Western cities where the railroad arrived before the settlement had attained any considerable size or industrial complexity, rail terminals preempted central sites and preceded the initial development of specialized commercial and industrial quarters.[18] The extremely fast growth of many interior cities, which was followed by the arrival of complementary or competitive rail links, often resulted in the emergence of several well separated terminal districts, and the intra-urban transfer problems thus created remained considerable until connecting lines were developed later in the century. In cities where extensive industrial growth and physical expansion preceded the arrival of the railroad, terminal construction close to centers of commerce and industry was possible only after existing buildings were demolished or new land was created by filling waterfront areas. Many companies, however, were confident of their ability to attract adjacent business and were satisfied with peripheral facilities. The terminals which served different sections of the local, regional, or national markets were frequently built in separate locations and thereby created a new set of problems. As long as the special facilities of the central areas were primarily concerned with regional distribution rather than local marketing, terminal arrangements aroused few objections, but toward the turn of the century inter-terminal transfers were identified as a major source of central urban congestion, which not only inconvenienced increasing numbers of commuters but also made it more difficult for local consumers to reach the central retail section.

These general observations are in part exemplified by the development of the land use pattern of central Boston between about 1840 and 1870. In 1840 specialized commercial and industrial land use was confined to several small and separate areas in the central part of the city, which at that time still housed a considerable resident population (Fig. 3-2). In the following years the food markets and the local administrative and financial quarters all increased in size, but the construction of warehouses for commercial and industrial activities accounted for the largest additions to the emerging central business district. By 1870 Boston's downtown, like that of most other American cities, was dominated by large warehouses and new premises for financial activities, although some parts of the quarter were devoted to the retail carriage trade. Between

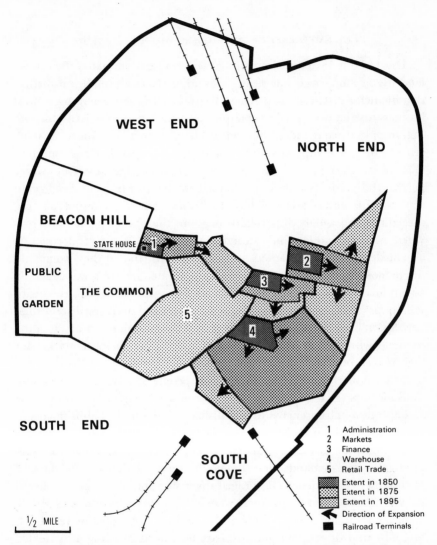

FIG. 3-2. The Expansion of Boston's Central Business District, 1850-1900

1835 and 1855 seven railroad terminals were established but apparently exerted only limited influence on the emerging central land use pattern. Although the two clusters of terminals attempted to locate close to the center by filling waterfront land in the Mill Pond and South Cove, they were still at a considerable distance from the advancing fringe of the business quarter (Fig. 3-2).

THE EMERGENCE OF THE MODERN BUSINESS DISTRICT

Until about 1870 multi-functional warehouses dominated the central land use of most large American cities, and, although small but distinctive financial districts had been well established, the emerging central business district would have been quite unfamiliar to a modern observer. Yet, in only three decades, the central business district assumed its modern extent and complexity. In particular, the expansion and improvement of streetcar services and the increased purchasing power of a large part of the urban population sustained the growth of specialized retail activities in central areas. Before 1870 most general retailing was unspecialized and widely dispersed throughout the city. General stores provided essential staples, and, although perishable foods were frequently obtained from central markets, peddlers also distributed these commodities in most sections of the city.[19] Centrally located retailing was generally an adjunct activity of both contract workshops primarily concerned with skilled tasks and warehouses designed to meet the needs of distant markets. Specialized retail shops already served the custom needs of a wealthy clientele while wholesalers had begun to cultivate a local market for their mass-produced goods. After about 1870, however, the increasing size of the local market and the willingness of people to travel to central locations for apparel, hardware, or drugs encouraged many more wholesalers and also new entrepreneurs to establish separate retail establishments.

Yet the emergence of a separate and extensive retail district awaited the organization of variety and department stores.[20] The market for mass-produced goods demanded less commodity specialization and for the sake of customer convenience encouraged diversification of the goods offered for sale. Thus, department stores were able to combine in one establishment the local sale of goods previously obtained from separate retail outlets. The new dimensions and diversity of central retailing also yielded economies of scale, which deepened the mass market for non-staple items by lowering prices as well as encouraging the development of variety or dimestores that offered a wide range of cheap items. This process was compounded by a secular decline in retail prices during the 1880's which prompted many manufacturers to cultivate the buying departments of large-scale retail stores in order to avoid the costs of commission agents and jobbers.[21] By advertising brand names and providing franchises for marketing, the manufacturers of mass-produced goods stimulated the

Downtown at the Turn of the Century

Boston's Retail Center, Washington Street, *c.* 1889
From Boston, Its Commerce, Finance and Literature, *New York, 1889*

Boston's Specialty Retail Quarter, Tremont Street, *c.* 1889
From Boston, Its Commerce, Finance and Literature, *New York, 1889*

Boston's Wholesale Warehouses, Sumner Street, *c.* 1889
From Boston, Its Commerce, Finance and Literature, *New York, 1889*

Boston's Food Markets, Faneuil Hall and Quincy Markets, *c.* 1889
From Boston, Its Commerce, Finance and Literature, *New York, 1889*

Central Congestion, Chicago, Randolph and Dearborn Streets, *c.* 1910
Courtesy Chicago Historical Society

growth of the retail sector at the expense of the wholesale sector of urban commerce. The new retail enterprises built new stores to display their wares and quickly assumed a dominant place in and around the nodal points of the local transportation system.

The enlarged urban market also encouraged large-scale specialty retailing in central locations because the demand for high-value and luxury goods justified spacious showrooms well separated from finishing or manufacturing areas. Such enterprises were less sensitive than department stores to the need to locate in easily accessible areas; instead they valued sites close to hotels or financial districts or high-income residential areas, all of which attracted a well-heeled clientele. Indeed, a substantial proportion of the growing custom of department stores was derived from the increasing number of commuters who found employment in finance, government, and local distributing. After about 1870 the organization of both the national and the urban economy was increasingly dominated by large-scale financial rather than industrial entrepreneurs. To serve the needs of "finance-capitalism," banking and insurance facilities multiplied, compounded by the expansion of a wide range of related activities such as real estate, brokerage, and legal and accounting functions.[22]

Like the warehouse quarter in earlier decades, the greatly enlarged financial districts began to handle the regional and national linkages of the urban economy. In larger cities these districts were not only redeveloped but they also expanded into adjacent premium locations—often at the expense of long-established commercial premises. Although this expansion, as well as the emergence of a central retail district, involved the construction of new taller buildings, the areal growth still encroached upon the warehouse facilities, which in turn compensated for their losses by continuing to invade adjoining residential quarters. Boston's central business district between about 1870 and 1900 illustrates the changes in central urban land use discussed in the preceding paragraphs. Most notable was the emergence of a large and separate downtown retail area (Fig. 3-2), and, although during that time new warehouses were built, buildings devoted to finance displaced many of the more centrally located warehouses.

Although direct dealing between manufacturers and retailers reduced the use of warehouses for marketing, high-value and infrequently needed items continued to attract buyers from a wide area who preferred to inspect a variety of goods in a wholesale warehouse. Local food retailers also continued to obtain their supplies from wholesalers, and the marketers of fresh produce, in particular, remained in central locations in spite of the age and inconvenience of their markets and the diseconomies of congestion.[23] The minute fragmentation of marketing combined with the unpredictable but frequently marginal profits discouraged ambitious efforts to improve the market structures or to change their locations.

As wholesale activities concentrated in warehouses in the most easily reached parts of the business district and as the growing spatial needs of finance and retailing increased land values, small-scale manufacturing was forced to seek new facilities on the advancing edge of the business district or in completely new locations. Partly because of the increasing spatial demands of other businesses, expanded production in manufacturing stimulated readjustments in scale, technology, and location. Some workshops, as in the footwear industry and branches of the furniture industry, sought new factory space and integrated several complicated production processes, thereby reducing their dependence on central locations.[24] Not all of the industries that abandoned the urban core relocated in the same area, however, for with the emergence of national markets access to raw materials or to major markets became important factors in business reorganization. During this period satellite cities and industrial suburbs were developed to accommodate the growing number of large-scale industries, creating a situation in which a limited number of plants dominated local employment rather than a seemingly infinite number of varied enterprises.[25] Before about 1900 decentralization in established cities was limited and the rapid spread of the construction and food-processing industries was largely responsible for the growth of suburban employment.

Certainly in metropolitan centers several major industries tenaciously clung to their central locations. The telephone reduced some of the locational restraints on businesses dependent on a rapid response to variable demands or to specific customer instructions, but the fragmentation of production still tied many enterprises to central locations. Most sections of the printing and publishing industries expanded rapidly but generally by multiplying small scale operations near to or within the central business district.[26] In the clothing industry, the contract system remained dominant because merchants relied on outside shops for almost the entire production.[27] Contracting for semiskilled and skilled tasks was particularly encouraged by the fact that Russian Jewish immigrants in many large cities found jobs in the manufacture of clothing, especially women's apparel. Eventually the initial contractor not only organized the sub-contracting for unskilled work but also assumed jobbing functions as the retail distributor tried to trim costs by avoiding the wholesale merchants. The industry expanded in tenements next to the central business district, and sweatshop production methods eventually prompted legislation which removed operations from living quarters.[28] However, workshops were then established in converted tenements or in fractional space in commercial buildings, and the contract system remained unchanged. The separation of production from design and marketing in both the clothing and printing industries became common only after about 1920, when local transport became more flexible.

Thus after about 1850 most of the expanding commercial and manu-facturing activities adopted central locations, and created several special-ized land uses in the urban core. A small cluster of warehouses and finan-cial facilities had expanded and become the components of the modern central business district, with interspersed and adjacent areas devoted to manufacturing. Warner suggests that it was "manufacturing that gave the early nineteenth century downtown its size and bulk. The downtown of 1860 was not as it is today, a mere creature of offices and stores."[29] Until about 1870 the concentration of urban employment in commerce and manufacturing stimulated the rapid expansion of multi-functional warehouses rather than more specialized accommodations. As executive and managerial functions were gradually divorced from production and distribution, the financial district became more important to the metro-politan and national economy. By about 1900 financial and related ac-tivities not only employed a rapidly growing segment of the urban labor force but also had enlarged their facilities in the most highly valued cen-tral locations, often at the expense of older commercial premises. The fast growth and increased purchasing power of the urban population also expanded and deepened the local market, and accordingly a retail dis-trict composed largely of department and variety stores claimed one of the largest segments of the central business district during the last dec-ades of the nineteenth century. Since access to local consumers was their most important locational consideration, most retail activities attempted to obtain sites near the nodal points of the streetcar systems.

Because of the new preeminence of financial and retail activities and the increasing concentration of warehouses on wholesale trade, central locations became more costly and less attractive to manufacturing. In an effort to retain agglomeration economies and access to local and distant markets, most urban manufacturers held on to their central sites, but rising costs caused by increased crowding continued to be a problem.[30] Attempts were made to reduce tie-ups by constructing elevated tracks, subways, or circumferential railroads between separate terminals, but, until trucks drastically reduced transport costs and automobiles and buses permitted a more flexible journey to work, decentralization offered few advantages to most centrally located enterprises. With the extensive use of high-rise construction within the central business district and the growth of new suburban centers of commerce and manufacturing since about 1920, the extent and internal differentiation of central concentrations of employment in many large cities represents an inheritance from nineteenth-century urban growth.

NOTES

1. R. M. Haig, "Towards and Understanding of the Metropolis," *Quarterly Journal of Economics,* 40, 1926, pp. 179-208.
2. R. M. Hurd, *Principles of City Land Values,* New York, 1903, pp. 56-59.
3. W. Alonso, *Location and Land Use,* Cambridge, 1964, pp. 8-9.
4. A. R. Pred, "The Intrametropolitan Location of American Manufacturing," *Annals, Association of American Geographers,* 54, 1964, pp. 165-80.
5. R. Turvey, *The Economics of Real Property: An Analysis of Property Values and Patterns of Use,* London, 1957, pp. 22-23; J. Rannells, *The Core of the City,* New York, 1956, pp. 35-50.
6. E. M. Hoover and R. Vernon, *Anatomy of a Metropolis,* Cambridge, 1959, pp. 62-73.
7. L. S. Moses and H. F. Williamson, Jr., "The Location of Economic Activity in Cities," *American Economic Review,* 57, 1967, pp. 211-22.
8. J. E. Vance, Jr., "Labor-Shed, Employment Field, and Dynamic Analysis in Urban Geography," *Economic Geography,* 36, 1960, pp. 189-220; D. Ward, "The Industrial Revolution and the Emergence of Boston's Central Business District," *Economic Geography,* 42, 1966, pp. 152-71; E. M. Hoover and R. Vernon, *op. cit.,* pp. 21-109. J. E. Vance, Jr., *Geography and Urban Evolution in the San Francisco Bay Area,* Berkeley, 1964, pp. 9-47. A forthcoming article by Martyn Bowden, "Laissez-faire Growth of the Central Districts of Large Cities: Some Preliminary Findings," based upon City Directory information offers a more precise examination of the emergence of specialized commercial land uses.
9. C. Bridenbaugh, *Cities in Revolt: Urban Life in North America: 1743-1776,* New York, 1955, pp. 250-91.
10. S. E. Morison, *The Maritime History of Massachusetts, 1783-1860,* Cambridge, 1961, pp. 160-212; R. G. Albion, *The Rise of New York Port, 1815-1860,* Hamden, 1939, pp. 213-34.

11. A. R. Pred, "Manufacturing in the American Mercantile City: 1800-1840," *Annals Association of American Geographers,* 56, 1966, pp. 307-38.
12. G. R. Taylor, *The Transportation Revolution,* New York, 1951, pp. 211-20.
13. B. E. Hazard, *The Organization of the Boot and Shoe Industry in Massachusetts Before 1875,* Cambridge, 1921, pp. 59-63.
14. J. Pope, *The Clothing Industry in New York,* Columbia, Mo., 1905, p. 7; O. Handlin, *Boston's Imigrants, A Study in Acculturation,* Cambridge, 1959, pp. 74-77.
15. E. C. Kirkland, *Industry Comes of Age,* New York, 1961, pp. 262-66; T. Marburg, "Domestic Trade and Marketing," in H. F. Williamson, ed., *The Growth of the American Economy,* New York, 1951, pp. 511-31.
16. H. M. Mayer, *The Railway Pattern of Metropolitan Chicago,* Chicago, 1943.
17. D. Ward, *op. cit.,* pp. 155-56.
18. A. Pred, *op. cit.,* 1964, pp. 167-68.
19. T. Marburg, *op. cit.,* pp. 511-31.
20. J. E. Vance, Jr., "Emerging Patterns of Commercial Structure in American Cities," in K. Norborg, ed., *Proceedings of the IGU Symposium in Urban Geography,* Lund, 1962, pp. 485-518; P. H. Nystrom, *Economics of Retailing,* Vol. 1, New York, 1915, pp. 125-73; R. M. Hower, *History of Macy's of New York, 1858-1919,* Cambridge, 1943, pp. 141-56, 231-53.
21. E. C. Kirkland, *op. cit.,* pp. 266-69; U.S. House Document, No. 183, 57th Congress, 1st Session, Serial No. 4344, *Report of the Industrial Commission,* 14, Washington, D.C., 1901, pp. xii-xiv.
22. E. M. Hoover and R. Vernon, *op. cit.,* pp. 84-94.
23. U.S. Federal Trade Commission, *Report on the Wholesale Marketing of Food,* Washington, 1920, pp. 114-50; Edwin G. Nourse, *The Chicago Produce Market,* Boston and New York, 1918, pp. 14-26, 71-91.
24. E. M. Hoover, "The Location of the Shoe Industry in the United States," *Quarterly Journal of Economics,* 47, 1933, pp. 254-76.
25. G. R. Taylor, *Satellite Cities: A Study of Industrial Suburbs,* New York, 1915.
26. R. B. Helfgott, "Women's and Children's Apparel," in M. Hall, ed., *Made in New York,* Cambridge, 1959, pp. 47-52.
27. W. E. Gustagson, "Printing and Publishing," in M. Hall, ed., *Made in New York,* Cambridge, 1959, pp. 137-54.
28. U.S. Senate Document, No. 2309, 32nd Congress, 2nd Session, Serial No. 3140, *Report of the Committee on Manufactures on the Sweating System,* Washington, D.C., 1893, pp. 227-31.
29. S. B. Warner, Jr., *The Private City,* Philadelphia, 1967, p. 58.
30. E. E. Pratt, *Industrial Causes of Congestion of Population in New York City,* New York, 1911.

4 IMMIGRANT

RESIDENTIAL QUARTERS

The central concentration of urban employment after about 1850 strongly influenced the location and characteristics of the residential areas of new immigrants, most of whom sought low-cost housing close to their places of employment. People of foreign birth soon dominated the central residential quarters, and, although there was considerable mixing of ethnic groups, members of each major group usually concentrated in one area, eventually identified as a ghetto. These central concentrations of low-income groups contrasted strikingly with the peripheral location of the poor in pre-industrial cities.[1] Under the conditions of a petestrian city, the rich lived in central areas—for convenience as well as for the prestige that came with living close to the city's political and religious institutions—and the immigrant poor tended to squat near the edge of town. Before the Industrial Revolution, the very rich often had developed small and exclusive residential sections beyond the city limits. But with the first signs of industrial and commercial development in the center, they accelerated their outward movement. The lack of transportation, however, greatly restricted suburban residence, and only after adequate systems had been developed were middle-income people able to leave central areas for peripheral sites. The vacated residences were then subdivided to provide cramped housing for new immigrants near to the growing sources of employment.

The first major influx of foreign immigrants took place before either urban employment had been centralized or local transportation had been improved; consequently, the residential pattern of the mid-nineteenth-century American city was transitional between pre-industrial and modern. Before the Civil War, Irish and German immigrants concentrated in central locations abandoned by more prosperous residents, but this source of housing served only a small part of the total influx. Others had to seek accommodation and employment in almost every section of the city, and many squatted in peripheral "shanty-towns," which were displaced only after the Civil War when streetcar systems opened new areas to middle-income development. At the same time, businesses also made claims on adjacent residential areas, and, although these areas were expanding outwards, most later immigrant arrivals were housed on the immediate edge of the central business district—by increasing the density of buildings and the number of people in each building.

Indeed, the most frequent theme of past evaluations of immigrant residential districts was the mortal and socially pathological repercussion of congested and unsanitary housing conditions. These districts came to symbolize both material and social failure in urban America and were often erroneously identified with high rates of infant mortality, crime, prostitution, drunkenness, and various other symptoms of social ills. Thus it was assumed that the living conditions endured by immigrants undermined personal health and domestic morality. Furthermore, the tendency of immigrants of similar nationalities and religions to congregate in ghettoes was often regarded as a threat to the "Americanization" or assimilation of the newcomer. Sensitive observers argued that housing reform and the regulation of living conditions would remove the major causes of the social problems, but less optimistic observers were convinced that restricting the entry of the more recent (and apparently less desirable) immigrants would alone solve the basic causes of urban problems. The bulk of the literature on immigrant living conditions, therefore, was strongly influenced by the political polemics of housing reform or immigration restriction, and, although existing records provided detailed and often penetrating evaluations of ghettoes, they rarely isolated the generic from the purely local characteristics of their particular investigation.[2]

THE LOCATION OF IMMIGRANT RESIDENTIAL DISTRICTS

Yet observers were generally able to agree that most immigrants congregated on the edge of the central business district, which provided the largest and most diverse source of unskilled employment. Although local transportation was improved and extended, many immigrants had jobs with long and awkward hours and preferred a short walk to work. Almost all immigrant families depended on the wages of every adult member of the family; consequently, the multiplication of low individual commuter fares inflated transportation costs beyond the means of most low-income families.[3] The tenure of most unskilled occupations was also characteristically uncertain, and daily hiring was the common procedure in general laboring. Immigrants thus faced not only constant changes in the locations of their work,[4] but also frequent spells of unemployment, and under these circumstances convenient access to the central business district was almost a necessity for workers who periodically were forced to search for substitute employment. Suburban industrial districts also attracted many immigrants, and cheap housing was built nearby, but residential areas close to the city center supported far larger numbers of immigrants because of the variety of industrial and commercial employment available there. Only in specialized manufacturing cities, where concentrations of large-scale industrial plants frequently employed more people than the central business district, were substantially fewer immigrants housed in central areas.

The first generation of immigrants to arrive in American cities in large numbers often provided almost the entire labor force in certain activities of the central business district, for the tendency of individual groups to specialize was marked. Irish immigrants found employment in the warehouses and terminal facilities they had helped to build, while German immigrants worked in the sewing machine and consumer supply trades, which were housed in the upper stories of warehouses.[5] New arrivals from Italy in part replaced the Irish as general laborers and were attracted to distributing fresh food from the central wholesale markets.[6] Jewish immigrants, equipped with long experience in the handicraft industries and the local commercial life of Eastern Europe, quickly developed many branches of merchandising at a time when the retail and wholesale segments of marketing were firmly established as distinct and specialized areas in the central business district.[7] Members of this group also rapidly took over the ready-made clothing industry, and, although they diverted production from warehouses to residential premises, the credit and informational needs of the industry still demanded locations with ready access to the central business district. Also, many of the immigrant businesses, which originally provided only for the distinctive material or dietary needs of the immigrant community, eventually expanded to serve far wider urban, regional, and national markets.

The residential fringe of the central business and manufacturing districts also indirectly provided by far the largest supply of cheap housing in most cities, for the threat of commercial and industrial expansion encouraged families whose income and working hours permitted a longer journey to work to abandon central residential areas. Before abandoned dwellings were demolished, the single-family houses were usually converted into multi-family tenements and their rear yards or surrounding grounds were filled with cheap new structures. Apartments rented at rates appropriate to the low incomes of most immigrants, but overcrowding, dilapidated structures, and unsanitary living conditions made even low rents exorbitant. Since the rents for units providing minimum housing needs were far beyond the means of most immigrants, few satisfactory low-rent structures were built.

Yet not all centrally located residential districts were taken over by immigrants immediately after the departure of the previous residents. In particular, spacious houses once belonging to the wealthiest members of the middle class were often utilized as lodging houses for single professional and clerical workers. Generally, these houses were further removed from the edge of the central business district than were the tenement districts, and it was assumed that converting them to lodging houses would not only maintain the status of the area, but would also be less costly than conversion to multi-family units.[8] These dwellings were the only centrally located housing available to black Americans when they arrived in northern cities in large numbers after about 1900.[9] The ratio of plumbing to rooms made the houses unsuitable for multi-family occupancy, but by then all alternative central and low cost housing had been preempted by European immigrants.

Most central residential districts, however, had been vacated on the assumption that demolition and commercial redevelopment would proceed quite rapidly. Thus capital improvements to the dwellings during the period of initial immigrant occupancy were extremely limited. But, there were often unanticipated delays in the expansion of commerce or industry, and, with the continued arrival of large numbers of immigrants, dilapidated tenements were demolished or removed to the rear of the lot and new multi-story structures were built on the vacant space. In older eastern cities, and especially in New York, the complete redevelopment of an entire lot with a five- or six-story structure was common, but in newer cities the relocation of the original building and the construction of two- to six-family tenements in the remaining space was the usual course. In cities with limited amounts of older housing, low-cost dwellings were constructed on newly platted land, and frequently drainage problems and the lack of adequate utilities rather than housing density created the major difficulties. Yet it was the construction of multi-story tenements for large numbers of families that excited the greatest popular concern in the late nineteenth century, and new minimum housing standards were designed, primarily to prevent the overcrowding of lots with tall structures. Because the new standards increased construction costs, rents in the improved buildings were often too expensive for low-income immigrants, and they continued to seek accommodation in older structures.[10]

THE INTERNAL SPATIAL STRUCTURE OF IMMIGRANT DISTRICTS

Living conditions

Although the common material deficiencies of the immigrant residential districts attracted considerable publicity and legislative activity, living conditions in these areas varied conspicuously both in quality and in the effects they had on the vital rates of the resident populations. Evaluations of conditions at the time emphasized the physically debilitating effects of overcrowded housing; nevertheless, local exceptions to the assumed relationship between mortality or morbidity and congestion aroused great curiosity. Although newly arrived immigrants tended to live in more cramped quarters than more established groups, the overall death rate of the populations of foreign birth were frequently somewhat lower than those of foreign parentage. The age structures of the newer immigrant groups, however, were dominated by vigorous young adults, whereas the earlier groups included large numbers of both very young and old people. Thus, although many earlier groups had moved into less crowded and often better housing, their more balanced age structures exposed them to the inflationary effects of higher death rates among infants and older adults.[11]

Yet age structure alone failed to explain strong contrasts in the death rates of groups with similar proportions of people of foreign birth and parentage. Russian-Jewish and Italian immigrants, for example, often lived alongside each other in extremely congested quarters, and, although the greater prevalence of family immigration among the Jews supposedly made them more vulnerable to infant mortality, such rates among the Russian-Jews were often the lowest in the city, whereas among Italians they were often nearly the highest. Most observers attributed the low death rates to the urban ancestry of Jewish people who, unlike most other immigrant groups, had made their adjustments to slum conditions long before arriving in American cities. In particular, there was an extremely low death rate among Russian Jews from pulmonary tuberculosis, one of the leading causes of death in the crowded areas; this immunity was shared by their co-religionists in European cities.[12] Some authorities attributed the extremely high death rate of Italians to dietary deficiencies and lack of familiarity with the severe American winter.[13] Even longer established immigrant groups also exhibited sharp contrasts in their mortality characteristics. People of Irish birth and parentage were afflicted with unusually high death rates throughout the nineteenth century, and tuberculosis, in particular, was more prevalent than among other immigrants who had arrived during the same period.[14] Finally, mortality rates were frequently high among people of native parentage who lived in immigrant neighborhoods because they were either the oldest or the most impoverished remaining members of the earlier resident group.

In spite of these demographic and ethnic considerations, most authorities rarely identified the spatial implications of the relationship between congested living conditions, high mortality, and large numbers of different ethnic groups and generally assumed that within the city high population density, high death rates, and high proportions of immigrants exhibited identical rather than separate distributions. On the basis of data for New York City and Brooklyn in 1890, it has been possible to demonstrate that high age-standardized death rates and a high population density per built-up acre occurred in quite separate locations which were associated with different ethnic groups.[15] For example, the population of Russian-Jewish parentage was strongly associated with high density and that of Italian parentage with high mortality, although the association was somewhat weaker. Earlier immigrant groups were not clearly connected with either high density or high mortality, and the ethnically more diverse districts occupied by long-established groups probably obscured a frequently publicized association between Irish populations and high mortality.

To summarize, a descriptive model of immigrant districts might show high mortality rates, a high population density, and proportionately large populations of immigrants as circles which occupy largely separate

Varieties of Immigrant Housing

New York's Tenements, Hester Street, *c.* 1905
Brown Brothers

New York's Shanty Towns, 91st Street at Fifth Avenue, *c.* 1898
The J. Clarence Davies Collection, Museum of the City of New York

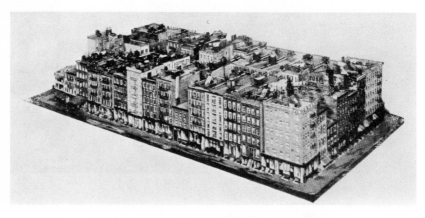

Block of Tenements, New York, *c.* 1900
From The Tenement House Problem, *New York, 1903*

Court Tenements, Boston, *c.* 1900
From The Tenement House Problem, *New York, 1903*

Row Houses, Philadelphia, *c.* 1900
From The Tenement House Problem, *New York, 1903*

HUNT LIBRARY
CARNEGIE-MELLON UNIVERSITY

Intermixed Single and Multi-Family Housing, Chicago, *c.* 1900
From Tenement Conditions In Chicago, *Chicago, 1901*

Alley Housing Behind Tenements, Chicago, *c.* 1900
From Tenement Conditions In Chicago, *Chicago, 1901*

but occasionally overlapping locations within a large city (Fig. 4-1). Areas which are described by different combinations of more than one of the three most widely publicized characteristics of immigrant quarters indicated above record the effects of distinctive ethnic groups. Area A describes districts with all three characteristics and represents the worst sections of the Italian ghetto; Area B, extremely crowded districts but ones with low death rates—clearly the Russian Jewish ghetto; and Area C, less congested sections with high mortality, representing earlier and frequently Irish immigrant groups. Area D, which combines high mortality and high density, describes remnant and impoverished populations of native parentage.

Quite apart from the different adjustments of ethnic groups to their housing environment, the rapid improvements in sanitation, piped water supply, and building practices changed the quality of the urban environment. At a time when housing reformers were publicizing the mortal or morbid consequences of congestion, others were popularizing the impact of sanitary engineering on the secular decline in urban death rates.[16] The paradox of declining death rates and increasing congestion could perhaps have been resolved if declining mortality had been confined to the expanding suburban districts, but some of the most spectacular reductions

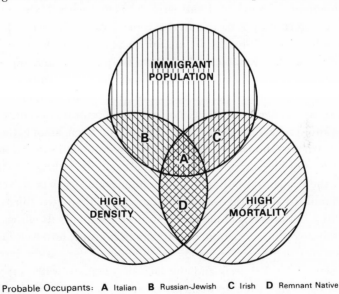

Probable Occupants: **A** Italian **B** Russian-Jewish **C** Irish **D** Remnant Native

FIG. 4-1. Model of the Internal Spatial Structure of Immigrant Residential Districts, 1890

in local death rates took place in overcrowded districts where sanitary conditions had improved. The material rewards of sanitary improvement, however, did not extend to all areas occupied by immigrants, for the arrangement and site conditions of the housing they inherited often defied attempts to improve the surroundings. Districts which originally had been developed as either individual dwellings set in spacious lots or as row houses with substantial front and rear grounds were swamped by cheap new structures in the form of rear tenements or of virtually inaccessible courts. Most sanitary facilities and utilities were confined to the public streets, and little attempt was made to alter this arrangement in the new buildings. The size of the original single-family residences also influenced living conditons, for large houses were frequently subdivided without the addition of new plumbing.

Local site conditions also strongly influenced sanitary improvements. For example, low-lying areas with saturated subsoil remained major centers of unsanitary living conditons. Wherever possible, shallow waterfront locations and local water bodies had been filled to create new land for both commercial and residential developments. Until about the mid-nineteenth century, there were no restrictions on the composition or the subsequent topography of the fill; thus buildings were often constructed on inadequate base material and were associated with threats to public health which could not be removed except by expensive redevelopments of entire localities.[17] Finally, the unsanitary practices of slaughter houses, breweries, and horse stables, which were frequently found side by side with immigrant housing, also influenced local living conditions.

For these reasons, it was possible for cities with neither extremely high-density residential districts nor extensive central concentrations of immigrants to have morbid living conditions. Even among the immigrant districts of the largest cities there was considerable variation in the proportions of high-density dwellings. For example, although more than half of the residential buildings in the immigrant districts of New York City contained more than six dwellings, more than two thirds of the residential buildings in Philadelphia were single-family dwellings (Table 4-1). In spite of these apparent advantages in housing, however, mortality rates in Philadelphia were among the highest in the nation, largely because of structural defects and the lack of adequate water supply and sewage disposal.[18] Immigrant districts in Chicago and St. Louis were characterized by large proportions of two- and three-family structures, but again structural defects and the neglect of sanitation created debili-

TABLE 4-1

Inter-City Contrasts in Immigrant Housing Characteristics, 1890

Per Cent Deviation of Each Individual City from the Mean for
All Six Cities: 1890

Families per Dwelling:	1	2	3	4	5	6	7-9	9+
Mean Per Cent	27.2	21.9	13.9	9.3	5.5	4.7	7.0	10.4
New York	−13.8	−14.9	−6.7	−2.7	0.0	0.8	8.9	28.5
Boston	−5.8	5.3	12.1	0.5	−0.4	−0.6	−2.6	−8.4
Philadelphia	39.1	−5.8	−6.2	−4.5	−3.3	−3.3	−5.9	−10.1
Chicago	7.5	3.4	1.1	2.8	−0.2	−0.8	−4.1	−9.7
Brooklyn	−9.4	1.0	4.0	2.1	4.5	4.7	2.7	−7.7
St. Louis	4.9	16.1	−2.3	0.9	−2.2	−2.4	−4.4	−8.8

Note: Statistics refer only to those wards with more than 70 per cent of their populations of foreign parentage.

tating living conditions. Since overcrowded and ill-ventilated rooms, poor water, and lack of sewerage and street-cleaning systems were the common discomforts of most immigrant districts, the selective effects of sanitary improvements within and between cities strongly influenced the morbid effects of the urban environment.[19]

Social characteristics

Congested living quarters were frequently regarded as a basic cause of not only high rates of sickness and death but also of social disorganization among immigrants. It was for long assumed that the behavior in many low-income immigrant neighborhoods was socially pathological and directly related to the breakdown of the traditional social organization of rural people in the impersonal and anonymous social environment of the city. Subsequent reevaluations of low-income neighborhoods have suggested that many observers failed to identify the presence of adequate and even elaborate social organization among immigrant populations largely because their behavior and priorities were different from those of suburban or native America.[20] Indeed, most newly arrived immigrants were hardly aware of the society of middle- and high-income native Americans with whom they were apparently expected to assimilate. Instead, their initial exposure was to earlier immigrant groups who had gradually gained control of segments of the political and economic life of many cities. Moreover, once a ghetto was established, it became in part a voluntary association. Most immigrants preferred to spend their early years in the city in a district where their fellow countrymen or co-religionists—often their friends and relatives—lived.[21] Under these circumstances, although few escaped the material and social discomforts of crowded living, some groups were able to avoid severe social disorganization and occasionally to attract laudatory, if often condescending, comments upon the stability and moral orthodoxy of their family and neighborhood life.[22] Although both legitimate and corrupt forms of political patronage excited popular condemnation, residential concentration provided large immigrant groups with proportionate shares of patronage at a time when public welfare was weakly developed.[23]

These social attractions and political advantages, however, were not shared by all immigrant groups nor did they exist in all central districts. Small groups not only lacked the numbers to support their own institutions but also rarely received their share of political patronage or jobs. Young single men living in rooming houses—those who hoped eventually to return home with the profits of American employment—were particularly affected, and their social predicament was often reflected in socially pathological behavior.[24] The age structure, sex ratio, and diverse ethnic characteristics of these quarters clearly distinguish them from those more typical immigrant ghettoes in which one or two large immigrant groups composed largely of families dominated extensive residential sections.[25]

THE EFFECT OF BUSINESS EXPANSION ON IMMIGRANT CONCENTRATION

Even the largest and most stable immigrant groups were unable, however, to establish enduring ghettoes in central fringe areas threatened by the continuous invasion of business premises. Different edges of the central business district expanded at different rates at different times, and this selective expansion of commercial premises was in part responsible for the variations in the living conditions and social characteristics of the central concentrations of immigrants. Early students of urban ecology emphasized the blighting effects of the central business district on adjacent areas and, in keeping with descriptions of these locations, concentrated upon their common material and social deficiencies.[26] Nevertheless, most ecologists acknowledged that the zone of blight was occasionally interrupted by high-income residences, and, subsequently, a sector arrangement of urban residential types was suggested to accommodate substantial variations in the rent levels.[27] The survival of both high-income districts and well organized ghettoes in central locations has been related to the sentiments and values of the occupants,[28] and, although these perspectives indicate more clearly the range of living conditions and social characteristics, their relationship to the selective and sequential emergence of different segments of the central business district remains obscure.

Both the rate and the extent of the advance of the business district clearly influenced the longevity of adjacent residential quarters and therefore, the material and social conditions of immigrants who settled there.[29] From the discussion of sequential expansion in Chapter 3, it is clear that on some margins of the central business district commercial activities followed so closely after the original inhabitants had left that newcomers had neither the time nor the incentive to establish a stable community (Fig. 4-2). These districts were occupied most frequently by the smallest or poorest immigrant groups along with the older and often more impoverished members of earlier groups that had moved on to better locations. Manifestations of social disorganization were thus rooted in the insecurity of residential tenure, frequent population turnover, and the failure of any one immigrant group to establish the institutional fabric of the ghetto. In contrast, other margins remained remarkably stable throughout the nineteenth century (Fig. 4-2). Where commercial

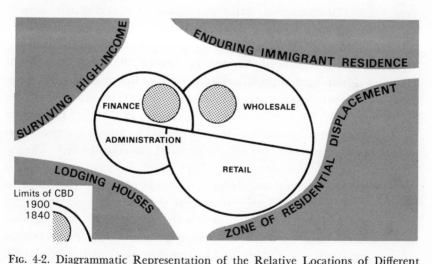

Fig. 4-2. Diagrammatic Representation of the Relative Locations of Different Central Residential Areas

encroachment was limited, for example, immigrants were able to establish enduring ghettoes and, indeed, areas which had initially been occupied by Irish and German immigrants eventually passed to Italian, Russian Jewish, and other later arrivals toward the turn of the century.

The selective characteristics of business expansion also allowed some
residents of adjacent districts to maintain their homes and, consequently,
influenced the location of surviving central high-income districts. Although site or historic status were the most frequently publicized advantages of central high-income districts, most large cities had several
alternative locations similarly endowed but which had capitulated to
immigrant settlement and business enchoachment. Yet one segment of
the central business district—the financial and administrative—attracted
rather than discouraged people of wealth and status (Fig. 4-2), and
throughout the nineteenth century many families highly valued living
close to the seats of financial and political power. Since this district provided decidedly limited opportunities for unskilled employment, the
demand for low-rent housing was much weaker than on margins adjoining the center of unskilled employment. Ecological theory clearly recog-
nized the spatial impact of the central business district on adjacent residential districts, but it should be noted that the impact was selective and,
therefore, responsible for the impressive variations in the material and
social conditions of this central residential zone.

The term "ghetto" frequently has been applied to concentrations of
poverty-stricken immigrants living in congested and segregated areas. It
has been suggested that the progressive enlargement and internal spatial
differentiation of immigrant areas limited the generic applicability of the
term to restricted parts of the city. Because of the limited supply of
abandoned housing and the dispersed pattern of urban employment, the
Irish and German immigrants who arrived in American cities before the
Civil War found housing in almost every section of the city. The largest
single immigrant concentrations were in central locations, but many also
settled in "shanty-towns" beyond the physical limits of the city. The ex-
pansions of streetcar systems in the 1870's and their electrification in the
1880's encouraged most middle-income people of native parentage to
leave central residential locations. During the same period the concentration of employment opportunities for immigrants in the central business district encouraged a proportionately greater central concentration
of new arrivals from southern and eastern Europe, and by about 1900
immigrants of diverse ethnic origins occupied extensive sections of the

inner city, while many established immigrants sought new accommodations in the inner suburbs.

Immigrants and their children thus accounted for a large, if not a dominant, proportion of the total populations of many large American cities; consequently, the concentration of particular ethnic groups in well defined districts separated them from other ethnic groups housed under similar circumstances rather than from a homogenous majority group. Moreover, the boundaries of ethnic ghettoes were seldom fixed or well defined and mixed ethnic popualtions lived in many immigrant districts.[30] Certainly the degrees of concentration of ethnic groups was not closely related to the quality of their living conditions nor was housing congestion closely related to their vital rates. Although ghettoes were frequently identified with the pathological social problems of urban society, certain advantages of residential concentration were also noted. The variable longevity and diversity of central immigrant concentrations, however, depended on the timing, scale, and direction of the expansion of adjacent non-residential land uses and on the appropriateness of the original housing for multi-family occupancy or a higher density of single-families. These conclusions are not intended to depreciate the amount of the discomfort endured by most immigrant families but rather to imply that the internal spatial structure rather than the common deficiencies of immigrant residential districts may well be more revealing of their generic characteristics.

NOTES

1. G. Sjoberg, *The Pre-industrial City,* New York, 1960, pp. 91-105.
2. E. E. Lampard, "American Historians and the Study of Urbanization," *American Historical Review,* 67, 1961, pp. 49-61.
3. F. H. Streightoff, *Standard of Living Among the Industrial People of America,* Boston and New York, 1911, pp. 22-28; United States Senate Document, No. 22, 62nd Congress, 1st Session, Serial 6082, *Cost of Living in American Towns,* Washington, D.C., 1911, pp. iv-v; E. E. Pratt, *Industrial Causes of Congestion of Population in New York City,* New York, 1911, pp. 116-85; H. L. Cargill, "Small Houses for Workingmen," in R. W. De Forest and L. Veiller, eds. *The Tenement House Problem,* Vol. 1, New York, 1903, pp. 331-32.
4. F. W. Streightoff, *op. cit.,* pp. 30-34.
5. R. Ernst, *Immigrant Life in New York City: 1825-1863,* New York, 1949, pp. 61-77; O. Handlin, *Boston's Immigrants,* Cambridge, 1959, pp. 54-87.

6. R. F. Foerster, *The Italian Emigration of our Times,* Cambridge, 1919, pp. 332-44; E. Lord, et. al., *The Italian in America,* New York, 1905, pp. 66-69.

7. S. Joseph, *Jewish Immigration to the United States from 1881 to 1910,* New York, 1914, pp. 42-46; C. S. Bernheimer, ed., *The Russian Jew in the United States,* Philadelphia, 1905, pp. 102-21.

8. A. B. Wolfe, *The Lodging House Problem in Boston,* Cambridge, 1913, pp. 9-14, 39-50.

9. G. Osofsky, *The Making of a Ghetto,* New York, 1967, pp. 105-49; E. F. Frazier, "Negro Harlem: An Ecological Study," *American Journal of Sociology,* 1937, pp. 72-88; A. H. Spear, *Black Chicago: The Making of a Negro Ghetto, 1890-1920,* Chicago, 1967, pp. 11-27.

10. L. Veiller, "Housing Conditions and Tenement Laws in Leading American Cities," in R. W. De Forest and L. Veiller, eds., *op. cit.,* pp. 129-72; E. E. Wood, *The Housing of the Unskilled Wage Earner,* New York, 1919, p. 25; C. Aronovici, "The Cost of a Decent Home," *Forum,* 58, 1914, pp. 111-12; R. Lubove, *The Progressives and the Slums,* Pittsburgh, 1962, pp. 217-56; J. Ford, *Slums and Housing,* Cambridge, 1936, pp. 72-204.

11. W. H. Guilfoy, "The Death Rate of the City of New York as Affected by the Cosmopolitan Character of its Population," *Quarterly Publications of the American Statistical Association,* 10, 1907, pp. 515-22; F. L. Hoffman, "The General Death Rate of Large American Cities: 1871-1904," *Quarterly Publications of the American Statistical Association,* 10, 1906-7, pp. 1-75.

12. M. Fishberg, "Health and Sanitation of the Immigrant Jewish Population of New York," *The Menorah,* 33, 1902, pp. 37-46, 73-82, 168-180; L. I. Dublin, "The Mortality of Foreign Race Stocks in Pennsylvania and New York: 1910," *Quarterly Publication of the American Statistical Association,* 17, 1920-21, pp. 13-44.

13. Kate H. Claghorn, "Foreign Immigrants in New York City," *Report of the Industrial Commission,* 15, 1901, pp. 449-91; R. Brindisi, "The Italian and Public Health," *Charities,* 12, 1904, pp. 443-504.

14. William H. Guilfoy, *op. cit.,* pp. 515-22; Kate H. Claghorn, *op. cit.,* pp. 460-61.

15. D. Ward, "The Internal Spatial Structure of Immigrant Residential Districts in the Late Nineteenth Century," *Geographical Analysis,* 1, 1969, pp. 337-53.

16. F. L. Hoffman, "American Mortality Progress During the Last Half Century," in Mazyck P. Ravenal, ed., *A Half Century of Public Health,* New York, 1921, pp. 94-117; G. E. Clark, "Sanitary Improvement in New York During the Last Quarter of a Century," *Popular Science Monthly,* 39, 1891, 319-30.

17. J. S. Billings, "Municipal Sanitation: Defects in American Cities," *Forum,* 15, 1893, pp. 304-10.

18. C. F. Wingate, "The City's Health—Sanitary Construction," *Municipal Affairs,* 2, 1898, pp. 261-70.

19. United States Senate Document, No. 338, 61st Congress, 2nd Session, Serial No. 5665, *Report of the Immigration Commission,* 1911, Vol. 66, *Immigrants in Cities,* Washington, 1911, p. 5.

20. W. F. Whyte, *The Street Corner Society,* Chicago, 1943, pp. 94-104, 255-278; H. J. Gans, *The Urban Villagers,* New York, 1962, pp. 3-41.

21. R. E. Park and H. A. Miller, *Old World Traits Transplanted,* New York, 1921,

pp. 60-80; C. F. Ware, *Greenwich Village, 1920-30*, Boston, 1935, pp. 3-8, 81-126; W. I. Thomas and F. Znaniecki, *Polish Peasant in Europe and America*, New York, 1927, pp. 1468-1546.

22. W. T. Elsing, "Life in New York Tenement Houses as Seen by a City Missionary," in R. A. Woods, ed., *The Poor in Great Cities*, New York, 1895, pp. 42-85; A. F. Sanborn, "The Anatomy of a Tenement Street," *Forum*, 18, 1894, pp. 554-72.

23. T. J. Lowi, *At the Pleasure of the Mayor: Power and Patronage in New York City: 1898-1958*, New York, 1964.

24. H. W. Zorbaugh, *The Gold Coast and the Slum*, Chicago, 1929, pp. 142-51; R. A. Woods, ed., *The City Wilderness*, Boston, 1898, pp. 33-57; E. Abbott, *The Tenements of Chicago: 1908-1935*, Chicago, 1936, p. 100.

25. G. C. Homans, *The Human Group*, New York, 1950, pp. 334-68; H. W. Zorbaugh, *op. cit.*, p. 129; W. I. Firey, *Land Use in Central Boston*, Cambridge, 1947, pp. 170-97, 290-313.

26. E. W. Burgess, The Growth of The City, in R. E. Park, ed., *The City*, 1925, pp. 47-62.

27. H. Hoyt, *The Structure and the Growth of Residential Neighborhoods in American Cities*, Washington, D.C., 1939.

28. W. I. Firey, "Sentiment and Symbolism as Ecological Variables," *American Sociological Review*, 10, 1945, pp. 140-48.

29. D. Ward, "The Emergence of Central Immigrant Ghettoes in American Cities: 1840-1920," *Annals of the Association of American Geographers*, 58, 1968, pp. 343-59.

30. *Report of the Immigration Commission, op. cit.*, pp. 6-8.

5 LOCAL TRANSPORTATION

AND SUBURBAN EXPANSION

As newly arrived immigrants were crowding into the central residential districts of American cities, considerable numbers of urban dwellers were moving into peripheral additions. New or improved local transportation made suburban residence possible for people who could afford better housing and whose shorter and more predictable working hours increased the time available for journey to work. Initially, these "dormitory" suburbs were small and exclusive, but by the turn of the century their inner sections accommodated substantial numbers of middle-income people, many of whom were established immigrants or their children. Some immigrant groups tended to cluster in specific suburban districts, but income and occupation as well as ethnic background and religion affected the choice of new locations. Between 1850 and about 1890, horse-drawn streetcars were the most important form of local transportation in American cites. The horse car moved at an average speed in the range between four and seven miles per hour, serving areas up to between two and three and a half miles of the city center, for, at the time, observers estimated that most commuters were prepared to spend a maximum of one hour per day getting to and from work in these conveyances.[1] When electrified services and rapid-transit systems were introduced during the 1880's, the average speed of local transport was more than doubled, thereby quadrupling the area within one half hour of the city center.

Although the potential extent of suburban growth was determined by successive improvements in local transportation, the actual residential additions were progressively diversified by changes in the demand for housing. The retrospective implications of some of the findings of urban ecology and land economics have provided insights into this process of growth and differentiation. Specifically, the tendency of high-income people to occupy spacious dwellings on the periphery of the city and for people of more modest means to live in more densely settled areas nearer to the major and usually central sources of employment has been related to the sequential physical expansion of the city.[2] The sequence was apparently initiated by people with high incomes who left their original dwellings for newer and more spacious ones on the edge of the city, thereby providing housing for people of more moderate means, whose own dwellings in turn were inherited by people of lower incomes. The most central dwellings were either demolished to make way for commercial expansion or were adopted by newly arrived immigrants.

With the growth of the total population and per capita wealth, each income group sought and generally found more attractive living quarters, often in areas already occupied by people of slightly higher incomes. They not only moved into vacated buildings but also into new ones that had been built on vacant or re-subdivided lots, which resulted in an outward movement of higher levels of population density. The original explanation of this process was based on analogies derived from plant ecology: the hypothesized zonal residential pattern of a city was attributed to the competitive process of invasion and succession whereby different income groups attained a dominance in different concentric zones around the city center.[3] On the assumption that most urban residents worked in the center of the city, sequential expansion and zonal differentiation were related to how much various income groups could afford for daily transportation. Thus, the zonal arrangement of income groups expressed gradations in the time and costs of local movement,[4] and innovations in urban transit not only enlarged the residential choices of each group but also accelerated the process of invasion and succession.

More recently Alonso has argued that, although invasion and succession was undoubtedly a major characteristic of urban expansion, an identical zonal arrangement of income groups would emerge if a city expanded too rapidly for the existing stock of vacated dwellings to meet the demands of low- and middle-income people.[5] Under these conditions, the zonal arrangement of residential areas was determined by the financial ability of a family to buy the house it preferred—even at the cost of a longer journey to work. Moreover, any concentric arrangement produced by invasion and succession assumes a regular outward expansion of the urban population. The physical enlargement of the city, however, was characteristically uneven and selective, so that at any given time a zone at a specified distance from the center might have been occupied by a wide range of income levels. Indeed, empirical studies have concluded that rent levels, housing quality, and indices of socio-economic status indicate a sector rather than a zonal arrangement. Hoyt, who initially proposed a sector model, argues that lines of transportation and the trends established by prestigious high-income groups encouraged a wedge-like expansion of different residential types, but that the precise mechanism whereby people of lower incomes responded to either the transportation system or the movements of high-income families remains unclear.[6]

Recent work in social area analysis and factorial ecology attempts to distinguish the locational patterns of household size and age structure from those of housing quality and socio-economic status.[7] Since the type and density of urban housing is strongly influenced by the decreasing unit cost of land with increasing distance from the city center, single-family dwellings big enough for large young families may only be obtained at some distance from the center. Although extreme poverty and racial or ethnic discrimination may exclude some groups from areas of spaciously arranged single-family housing, the size and age structure of urban households tend to reveal a zonal arrangement in which the largest and most youthful families occupy the most spacious and peripheral developments. Also, because the demographic characteristics of socio-economic groups differ, both property values and housing quality vary considerably within each zone. Indices of socio-economic status thus approximate to the sector arrangement Hoyt identifies. Although the residential areas of the wealthy may well have exhibited a sector-like pattern during the nineteenth century, the limitations of the streetcar system prevented most lower-middle and low-income families, whatever their size and age structure, from seeking the peripheral sites. The dominance of centrally located employment and the rapid decline in the frequency and density of streetcar service with increasing distance from the city center tended to encourage a zonal separation of all except the most affluent families.

In contrast to these geometric approximations, Firey suggests that the social ecology of the city did not assume any particular simple and well defined spatial pattern, stating that sentiments and values rather than cost minimizing or space maximizing considerations determined the continuity or stability of residential land uses over a considerable period of time.[8] Well defined districts within cities assumed a symbolic status in the value systems of particular social groups; consequently, the prestige or ethnic identity of an area provided enduring attractions, even though more spacious and convenient housing was available elsewhere in the city. Whereas traditional ecological generalizations attempt to relate present land use to the physical enlargement of the city, Firey demonstrates that land use, once established, tended to endure in spite of residential changes on the edge of the city. Although Firey notes how past conditions have directly influenced present land-use patterns, he does not elaborate on their extent and location, so that the relevance of his findings to changes in the residential structure of the city as a whole is difficult to determine. Indeed, his primary concern is with central land uses, which were long established before streetcar services altered the residential pattern of the city. Thus, the most historically rooted discussion of urban ecology does not address itself to peripheral expansion and, in order to identify the changing dimensions and forms of suburban growth, ecological generalizations need to be complemented by a sequential or developmental discussion of each major change in local transportation.

TRANSPORTATION CHANGES AND URBAN EXPANSION

Secular fluctuations in building activity provide a crude but useful record of how the rate of physical expansion in cities has varied. Although population growth, immigration and the competitive demands of alternative sources of investment strongly influenced construction throughout the nineteenth century, the peaks in building activity in the United States occurred during periods when transportation was improved or expanded.[9] Indeed, Isard has suggested that the 17- or 18-year cyclical movements in building were responses to new economic opportunities created by transportation innovations (Table 5-1).[10] Changes in inter-urban as well as intra-urban transportation contributed to each upswing in building, but toward the turn of the century improvements in local transportation had a far greater influence on the volume of construction. Isard associated canal and railroad construction with the peaks in building activity that occurred in 1836, 1853, and 1871. There were also related developments in local transportation, for limited railroad services were initiated in the mid-1830's, and horsecars were introduced in the early 1850's, followed by a substantial extension of their routes in the late 1860's. Peaks in the building cycle in 1890 and 1909

TABLE 5-1

Peaks and Troughs in the Building Cycle in the United States, 1830–1920

Peaks	Troughs
	1830
1836	
	1843
1853	
	1864
1871 (39.8)	
	1878 (16.3)
1890 (88.3)	
	1900 (49.3)
1909 (118.5)	
	1918 (24.6)

Note: Number of units started in brackets. 1929 = 100.

were identified with the electrification of street railways and the completion of rapid-transit systems.

Land subdivision and the sale of lots also exhibited a periodicity similar to the cycle of the building industry. At any given time, subdivided land prepared for sale occupied a more extensive and regular zone than did lots actually sold, and most cities possessed an oversupply of land subdivided and legally prepared for sale and development. Fellman, who has described pre-building growth patterns in Chicago, estimates that more than half of the city's present area was subdivided by 1871 and more than two thirds by 1885.[11] Although the land was far removed from any existing or proposed transportation routes, most of the subdivision took place during building booms. Lot sales were also heavily concentrated in the boom years, but often there was a lag between subdivision and sale: much of the newly parceled land would not be sold until the next upswing in building activity. For example, in Chicago the greatest amount of subdivision took place from 1866 to 1875, when more than one third of the city's land was prepared for sale. But the greatest volume of lots was sold from 1886 to 1895.[12] The location of newly subdivided areas in Chicago indicated no relationship with the routes of the local transport system. In contrast, lot sales did respond to the influence of new transportation lines, for in areas within a half mile of the horsecar routes almost one third of the land was sold in the three years preceding and the five years succeeding the establishment of the routes.

Cable cars and elevated transit lines had a more limited impact on lot sales, but these new services passed through areas already affected by the horsecar. Certainly, lot sales in Chicago during the second half of the nineteenth century provide some indication of the spatial as well as the temporal relationship between transportation changes and the anticipated physical expansion of the city.

Largely because of speculative anticipation of and delayed responses to innovations in transport, the degree of coincidence between upswings in the building cycle and the introduction of improved facilities was at best approximate. Local economic conditions strongly influenced both the timing and the amplitude of land sales and construction; thus, for the cities settled after the introduction of the horsecar, it is difficult to separate construction associated with the settlement and early growth from that stimulated by local transportation. The rapidly growing western cities tended to adopt streetcars earlier than eastern cities of comparable size, yet the major centers of the northeastern seaboard were first to adopt new transport systems on a large scale. Certainly, the outer limits and characteristics of the residential developments associated with each major improvement or extension of local transportation were remarkably similar in most of the largest cities of the nation.[13]

Middle-income developments in the peripheral areas of most cities began with the introduction of horsecars during the early 1850's. But in the northeastern seaports well-to-do merchants had built town houses in exclusive and often elevated locations since the late eighteenth century. Like their European and particularly their English counterparts, these men also purchased country estates within a half-day's journey from their urban residences and employment. The introduction of inter-urban steam railroads incidentally made it possible for some merchants to commute from their country estates. During the 1840's steam railroad companies established fares and schedules geared to the daily needs of wealthy commuters, and stations within a half hour from the city terminals became the nuclei of a discrete form of suburban development. Kennedy has documented the scale of early commuting in the Boston area, where in 1848 approximately 20 per cent of the men of business used the steam railroad for their journey to work.[14] Of a total of 208 passenger trains which arrived at or departed from the seven major terminals in the city, 118 served only stations within fifteen miles of central Boston. The majority of these stations were from twelve to fifteen miles from central Boston; consequently, their adjacent suburban developments were not only isolated from one another but also well separated from the contiguous built-up area of the city. Generally, a modified stage-coach or horse-omnibus served areas within ten miles of the city center but slow speeds and high fares made their use for commuting impossible.

The horsecar was introduced in the 1850's, and services expanded as steam railroads found it increasingly difficult to maintain commuter fares which even the wealthy could afford.[15] Indeed, later in the century legislation was approved requiring railroads to provide commuter services within the reach of the working man. Meanwhile, the horsecar—with its lower capital and operating cost, its more frequent stops, and its superior access to the urban core—encouraged residential development on the fringes of the city. Before the Civil War, however, the expansion was decidedly modest. Most companies operated on a single thoroughfare leading out of the city, and, if routes extended more than a half mile beyond the built up area, it was to reach real estate holdings owned by the company. The new developments also attracted some of the most prosperous members of the middle class, although they lived in large town houses arranged in terraced rows rather than in the typically suburban single-family houses set on separate lots. The surviving terraced brownstone rows of large eastern cities are an inheritance from this period when urbane building styles characterized the outward expansion of the city.[16]

Between the end of the Civil War and the depression of 1873, horse-car routes were extended into unremunerative territory, and, although there was an upswing in residential construction in the late 1860's, operating costs had increased and the growth in traffic was too small to support the capital costs of expansion.[17] During the 1870's and the 1880's, however, deflation reduced both capital and operating costs, and many of the lines were extended about four miles from the city center, which represented a journey of one half or three quarters of an hour.[18] Many of the extensions were initially designed to serve outlying hospitals, cemeteries, and parks. The weekend and holiday use of these lines sustained them until adjacent residential developments supported commuter services. Although separate single-family dwellings were now the dominant form of suburban housing, most new construction was confined to discontinuous ribbon development.

Warner has suggested on the basis of his study of Boston's southwestern suburbs that this ribbon development broadened to include areas within five minutes' walking distance of the horsecar route whenever there was service at less than five-minute intervals. Many of the original services to peripheral institutions or parks were infrequent or at non-business hours and unsuitable for commuting purposes.[19] Areas between the residential strips along the major routes were developed as crosstown and branch routes were built. Crosstown routes were particularly important in opening the suburbs to skilled workers whose place of work was not fixed, but by the late 1880's these routes extended only as far as two and a half miles from the city center. Beyond this distance, circumferential travel along crosstown routes would have increased the traveling time to work beyond the acceptable half hour and transfer costs would have inflated the fares of the people who could least afford it. In the large area between two and one half and four miles from the city, ribbons of upper-middle-income residences lined the major horsecar routes, and the interstitial areas remained largely untouched by residential developments (Fig. 5-1).

The rapid multiplication of spaciously arranged single-family housing was in part dependent on the relatively low land values of peripheral

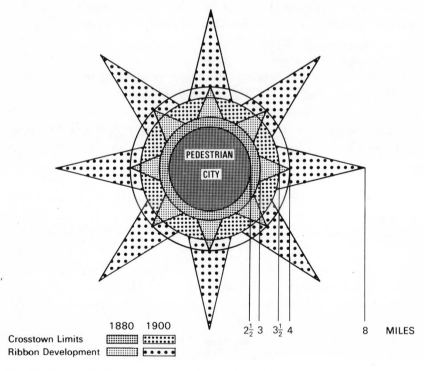

FIG. 5-1. Generalized Sequence of the Expansion of Streetcar Networks in American Cities, 1850-1910

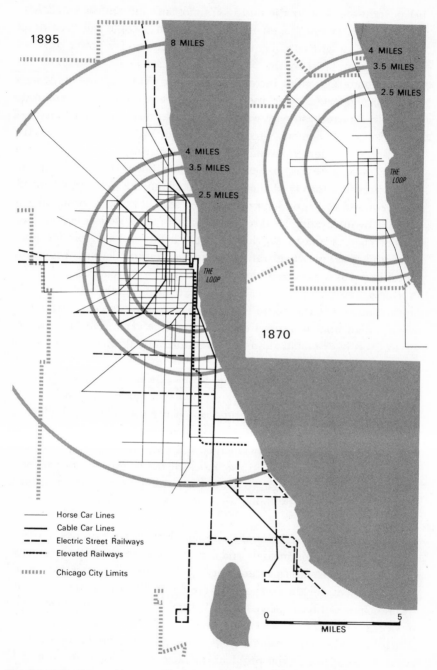

1895

8 MILES

4 MILES

3.5 MILES

2.5 MILES

THE
LOOP

1870

4 MILES

3.5 MILES

2.5 MILES

THE
LOOP

———— Horse Car Lines
———— Cable Car Lines
– – – Electric Street Railways
······· Elevated Railways
꘎꘎꘎꘎꘎ Chicago City Limits

0   5
MILES

FIG. 5-2. The Expansion of Chicago's Streetcar Network, 1870-1893

urban locations, but by the mid-1880's most of land within a half hour of the city center suitable for low-middle-income people had been developed for building. Experiments in changing the motive power of streetcars were stimulated by the prospect of increasing the "half-hour" distance without a parallel increase in the cost. Although steam, storage batteries, and cables were used to drive streetcars, electric power delivered by an overhead wire was rapidly substituted for other sources of power.[20] Initially demonstrated in Richmond, Virginia in 1887, electric streetcars were adopted by most large cities within a year. They were cheaper to operate per passenger mile than horsecars because of the larger carrying capacity of the rolling stock, but the high initial investment required for equipment often forced several horsecar companies to merge.[21] By integrating local services, the companies were able to abolish transfer charges and to provide unified schedules. Thus, the increased range and speed of urban transit systems was in fact derived from route coordination as well as from the use of electrically driven cars.

During the 1890's electrified services extended rapidly, and areas adjacent to routes as far as six to eight miles from the city center were now within a half hour of central employment. The expansion of crosstown services was less dramatic and more variable, but Warner indicates that in Boston their outer limits advanced by about one mile to three and a half miles from the city center (Fig. 5-1).[22] Chicago provides a good example of the changes in urban transit that took place between 1880 and 1890 when new sources of energy were being tested. Until 1880 most horsecar routes served areas within about four miles from the Loop, and crosstown routes had scarcely emerged (Fig. 5-2). By the early 1890's, although horsecars were still in use, much of the transit system had been electrified and reached eight to ten miles from the Loop. Crosstown lines, however, were generally limited to areas within three and one half miles from the center.

The upswing in residential building which peaked in most cities in 1890 was in part an immediate and sustained response to extended transit systems. Streetcar mileage continued to increase long after the initial building boom, for the companies were confident of creating new traffic by branching out into open country. Yet the swift expansion of electrified services compounded the growing problem of central urban congestion, which threatened to eliminate newly gained increments in speed. In an attempt to cope with the problem, elevated tracks were introduced in New York as early as 1878 and in Chicago in 1892, while in Boston a

The Changing Form of Local Urban Transportation: Chicago

Horse Omnibus, *c.* 1850
Courtesy Chicago Historical Society

Horsecar, *c.* 1858
Collection of George Krambles, Chicago

Steam-Dummy Railroad, *c.* 1865
The West Side Historical Society, Chicago

Cable Car, *c.* 1885
The West Side Historical Society, Chicago

Cable Car, 1882
Courtesy Chicago Historical Society

Electric Car, *c.* 1890
The West Side Historical Society, Chicago

Elevated Railroad, 1912-13
Collection of George Krambles, Chicago

combined subway and elevated system was opened in 1897. The capital costs of these improvements discouraged both private investment and public development, particularly after 1897 when inflation multiplied the cost of construction and operating. The street railroads themselves were frequently overcapitalized, partly because their original equipment had quickly become obsolete and partly because the lines extended far beyond the limits that traffic was able to support.[23] After the turn of the century, these financial difficulties were reflected in a decline in revenue per passenger mile, and it became clear that a uniform five-cent fare (the amount commuters apparently regarded an acceptable maximum) was no longer adequate to sustain a profitable enterprise.

After impressive beginnings in the late 1880's, electrified streetcar systems were greatly curtailed by financial problems. For the first two decades of the present century companies seemed unable or unwilling to improve their capital equipment, or to face the competition of motor buses and automobiles. Nevertheless, the extent of both the streetcar systems and the residential developments associated with them were unprecedented elsewhere in the urbanized world. Outside of the European capitals improvements in urban transportation were made considerably later than in the United States and then on a decidedly limited scale. For example, American cities with populations greater than 100,000 often had between 250 and 1,000 miles of track, while European cities with similar populations were likely to have only between 50 and 100 miles of track.[24] The fare structure in European cities was graduated according to the distance traveled and tended to restrict commuters to areas closer to the city center than did the uniform fares of American streetcars. Certainly, the extent of residential developments was much smaller, and single-family dwellings set within their own lots were extremely rare. Even in England, where domestic privacy was valued as highly as in the United States, terraced rows remained the dominant form of new middle-income dwellings. The limited extent of lines and graduated fare structures well may have restricted streetcar suburban developments in European cities, but the size of the middle-income population able to support suburban residence was also probably somewhat larger in American than in European cities.[25]

THE DIFFERENTIATION OF SUBURBAN RESIDENTIAL AREAS

Between the mid-1800's and the turn of the century suburban additions were transformed from small exclusive high middle-income developments into areas which housed almost all of the growing middle-income segment of the urban populations. Although the extension of streetcar systems had enlarged the potential extent of residential addition, the demand for land and housing in the new locations was largely dependent on the rates of social mobility. Certainly, home ownership was one of the most tangible results of social mobility, and, since most suburban housing was constructed for owner-occupiers, suburban growth became a compound product of spatial and social mobility. In 1900 only a small percentage of the total populations of large cities owned their own houses: 12 per cent in New York and about 25 per cent in Boston and Chicago (the latter percentage was more typical of the larger cities).[26] Quite apart from considerations of income, the spatial mobility of much of the urban population, both within and between cities, discouraged extensive home ownership. For example, although only one quarter of Boston's families actually owned houses in 1900, an equal proportion would eventually accumulate enough capital in their lifetimes to choose between ownership and tenancy.[27]

The desire or capacity of individual households to substitute mortgage and tax payments for rent, however, was not entirely dependent on increments to income derived from occupational mobility. After investigating the fortunes of unskilled manual laborers in Newburyport, Massachusetts between 1850 and 1880 Thernstrom suggested that occupational mobility was distinctly limited, but that real estate was readily available to laborers who remained in the town for any length of time.[28] Indeed, although employment was unpredictable and seasonable, frequently forcing many laborers to move from town to town, many of the people who stayed in one city were able to accumulate modest equities in real estate while they were still laborers. Moreover, the rates of home ownership were higher among immigrant laborers than among the second generation of immigrants, who themselves had higher rates of ownership than laborers with native-born parents. Yet the amounts and values of property owned by immigrants were usually small, indicating only a modest material and status advancement; for many households investment in a house and land was often at the expense of other opportunities for social mobility.[29] Although these findings were based upon data for only one city, Thernstrom presents a convincing evaluation of their applicability to American cities as a whole during the late nineteenth century. However, he does not discuss explicitly the relationship of his findings to the emerging residential structure of the city.

Warner proposes a useful distinction between inner suburban areas occupied by lower-middle-income families who were dependent on crosstown streetcar services and the more extensive outer zone of higher-middle-income households served by linear routes that extended well beyond the outer limits of the crosstown lines.[30] Among the people living in the inner suburban zone, it is possible that there were some who earned less than the average income for the area, but had accumulated savings during an extended period of residence. Thus, the rate at which the inner zone was occupied may have been as dependent on the number of families who had lived in a particular city for ten or twenty years as on the number able to afford a suburban dwelling at a given point in time. These inner suburbs were located between the outer edges of the pedestrian city of 1850 and the outer limit of the crosstown lines of 1900 and were originally occupied by upper-middle-income families who had moved on to more spacious locations. By 1900, however, only districts as far as approximately three and a half miles from the city center had adequate streetcar services for people with long or awkward working hours and shifting places of employment. In spite of the vast extension of the streetcar system most commuters were restricted to areas within the limits of crosstown services, and some residents of this inner zone were employed locally. Observers at the time continued to document the close relationship between working hours and the length of the journey to work long after the advent of electrified and rapid-transit commuter systems.[31]

Although some higher-income families stayed in the inner suburban zone, the process of invasion and succession prevailed throughout most of its extent. Housing characteristics changed gradually as modest single-family dwellings or small multiple-family units were constructed on vacant or re-subdivided lots. These structures were a notable improvement over the crowded tenements of the central parts of the city, but even then they were too cramped, and the surrounding areas lacked the amenities needed to fulfill the more saguine expectations of suburban life. Indeed, not only the physical characteristics but also the quality of family and social life in this "zone of emergence" troubled settlement-house workers who had hoped that immigrant families would find and create a more rewarding environment in moving from congested central quarters.[32] To some residents an inner suburban home was the ceiling of their material expectations, but to others it was only temporary, serving them until they were able to move to a better house in a more peripheral location. The turnover of the youthful and mobile population and the modest incomes of the residents of long standing were primarily responsible for the limitations of suburban living in these areas. Nevertheless, with some exceptions, living conditions were substantially better than in the central districts, and as centers of second generation or established immigrant families these districts supported impressive monuments to their religious identities.

In the initial move from the central ghettoes a large part of most immigrant groups tended to reconcentrate in particular districts, and, although some ethnic or national distinctions well may have diminished, the descendents of Catholic, Jewish, and Protestant immigrants usually settled different sections of the inner suburban area. Old World languages and customs were less prevalent than in the central ghettoes, but residual ethnic characteristics survived, increasingly defined by race and religious adherence.[33]

In many cities the original nucleus of the black ghettoes was located in the inner suburbs. There rooming and lodging houses, once the homes of the rich, were taken over—with little structural modification—for black residence. For many people, the inner suburbs represented only one stage in the outward movement from the central ghetto; for others, particularly black Americans, these badly deteriorating districts have become permanent residential quarters. Today Harlem most clearly exemplifies this type of development.[34]

Before 1920 very few people lived beyond the limits of the cross-town transit services because the lower density of the streetcar routes left large interstitial areas without adequate access to major sources of employment. The upper middle-income residents of these outer zones—most of them descendants of native-born white Protestants, but many members of established immigrant groups—generally had occupations with sufficient security to justify a mortgage. Clearly their original ethnic identity was less relevant to their residential choice than their income and occupation, so that observers confidently recorded the emergence of a society in which immigrants had assimilated. Yet before 1920, Catholic and Jewish families had not yet penetrated these areas in large numbers. Although extremely rich families also occupied parts of the outer zone, they were not necessarily in the most peripheral locations. Indeed, largely because these people were not dependent on public transportation, they tended to retain and to seek areas with desirable site properties or established status. Until 1920 high-income residential areas generally occupied a narrow wedge of land with a long established and prestigious central district at its apex.

Thus, the physical additions to the city made possible by successive improvements in local transportation were characterized by a better urban environment, which contrasted sharply with increasingly congested central areas. By 1900, however, the zonal structure of peripheral areas was well defined. It was composed of largely built-up inner suburbs occupied by lower middle-income people who relied on crosstown or frequent streetcar service and a partly developed outer zone of more prosperous residents living in spaciously arranged single-family dwellings. The transition between these two zones generally occurred at about three and one half miles from the city center, but age, topographic peculiarities, and population size resulted in some variation between different cities. The inner zone was first developed for upper-middle-income occupants during the heyday of horsecar services, and, although some affluent residents maintained particularly desirable residential quarters there, most of them moved on to newer houses when electrification expanded commuting ranges. For most urban residents the vacated houses of the well-to-do or new structures built on vacant or re-subdivided lots in the inner zone represented the ceiling of their expectations. Although the changing age structure and size of established immigrant families encouraged the movement to larger living quarters, the increasing pressure of newly arrived immigrants and the unsatisfactory living arrangements of most tenements pushed families of all sizes and ages from central areas. Similarly, very few outer suburban developments designed for large families were built for lower middle-income people. Differences between the inner and outer suburban zones largely reflected income and employment, for until the advent of the automobile and motor bus the limitations of the streetcar system insulated upper middle-income areas in the outer zone from invasion by less affluent people. By 1900, the inner suburbs did display considerable variations in the ethnicity and mobility of their populations, but the emergence of sector-like arrangements of socio-economic groups became more pronounced after about 1920 as a result of the more complete and diverse occupancy of the outer suburbs. Certainly, since that date many inner suburbs have lost their socially mobile residents and are now identified with the problems of central residential districts.[35]

NOTES

1. Massachusetts House Document, No. 475, 1898, *Report of the Special Commission on the Relation Between Cities and Street Railroad Companies,* Boston, 1898, p. 65, G. M. Smerk, "The Streetcar: Shaper of American Cities," *Traffic Quarterly,* 21, 1967, pp. 569-584.
2. E. W. Burgess, "The Growth of the City," in R. E. Park, ed., *The City,* Chicago, 1922, pp. 47-62.
3. *Idem.*
4. E. M. Hoover and R. Vernon, *Anatomy of a Metropolis,* Cambridge, 1959, p. 169.
5. W. Alonso, "The Historic and the Structural Theories of Urban Form: Their Limitations for Urban Renewal," *Land Economics,* 40, 1964, pp. 227-31.
6. H. Hoyt, *The Structure and the Growth of Residential Neighborhoods in American Cities,* Washington, D.C., 1939.
7. T. R. Anderson, "Social and Economic Factors Affecting the Location of Residential Neighborhoods," *Papers and Proceedings of the Regional Science Association,* 9, 1962, pp. 161-70; R. A. Murdie, "The Factorial Ecology of Metropolitan Toronto, 1951-1961: An Essay on the Social Geography of the City," *Department of Geography Research Paper No. 116,* Chicago, 1968.
8. W. I. Firey, *Land Use in Central Boston,* Cambridge, 1948.
9. J. R. Riggleman, "Building Cycles in the United States, 1875-1932," *Journal of the American Statistical Association,* 28, 1933, pp. 174-83.
10. W. Isard, "A Neglected Cycle: The Transport Building Cycle," *Revue of Economic Statistics,* 24, 1942, pp. 149-58; W. Isard, "Transport Developments and Building Cycles," *Quarterly Journal of Economics,* 57, 1942, pp. 90-112.
11. J. D. Fellmann, "Pre-Building Growth Patterns in Chicago," *Annals of the Association of American Geography,* 47, 1957, pp. 59-82.
12. *Idem.*
13. B. McKelvey, *The Urbanization of America, 1865-1915,* New Brunswick, 1963, pp. 75-79.
14. C. G. Kennedy, "Commuter Services in the Boston Area 1835 to 1860," *Business History Review,* 26, 1962, pp. 277-87.
15. *Idem.*
16. C. Tunnard and H. H. Reed, *American Skyline,* Boston, 1955, pp. 127-30.
17. E. S. Mason, *The Street Railway in Massachusetts,* Cambridge, 1932, pp. 3-6.
18. *Idem.*
19. S. B. Warner, *Streetcar Suburbs: The Process of Growth in Boston,* Cambridge, 1962, pp. 49-52.
20. H. H. Vreeland, "The Street Railways of America," in C. M. Depuir, ed., *One Hundred Years of American Commerce,* New York, 1895, pp. 141-48.
21. *Idem.*
22. S. B. Warner, *op. cit.,* pp. 61-62.
23. E. C. Mason, *op. cit.,* pp. 12-14.
24. Massachusetts House Document, No. 475, *op. cit.,* pp. 249-52.

25. D. Ward, "A Comparative Historical Geography of Streetcar Suburbs in Boston, Massachusetts and Leeds, England: 1850-1920," *Annals of the Association of American Geographers*, 54, 1964, pp. 477-89.

26. E. C. Kirkland, *Industry Comes of Age*, New York, 1961, pp. 258-59.

27. S. B. Warner, *op. cit.*, pp. 8-10.

28. S. Thernstrom, *Poverty and Progress: Social Mobility in a Nineteenth Century City*, Cambridge, 1964, pp. 117-37.

29. *Idem*.

30. S. B. Warner, *op. cit.* pp. 46-66.

31. E. E. Pratt, *Industrial Causes of Congestion of Population in New York City*, New York, 1911, pp. 116-85.

32. R. A. Woods and A. J. Kennedy, eds., *The Zone of Emergence*, Cambridge, 1962, pp. 1-2, 21-25.

33. N. Glazer and D. P. Moynihan, *Beyond the Melting Pot*, Cambridge, 1963, pp. 288-315; L. Rodwin, *Housing and Economic Progress: A Study of the Housing Experiences of Boston's Middle-Income Families*. Cambridge, 1961, 102-3.

34. G. Osofky, *The Making of a Ghetto*, New York, 1967, pp. 105-9; also cf. A. H. Spear, *Black Chicago: The Making of a Negro Ghetto, 1890-1920*, Chicago, 1967, pp. 20-27.

35. A forthcoming work by Peter G. Goheen, "Victorian Toronto, 1850-1900: Pattern and Process of Growth," *Department of Geography Research Paper No. 127*, Chicago, 1970, completed after this book was in press, provides a careful analysis and a sharper specification of many of the issues raised in this chapter.

POSTSCRIPT

This book has attempted to identify some of the locational aspects and implications of urban growth in the United States for roughly the hundred years following 1820. During that period the total population of the country increased more than tenfold to reach about 105 million in 1920. Natural increase was important in that growth, but the population was also greatly swollen by the arrival of more than 33 million immigrants. Since the majority of the new arrivals were young adults, their native-born children accounted for a large proportion of the natural increase. Immigrants were major contributors to the cityward movement, and by 1920, when slightly more than one half of the total population lived in settlements classified as urban by the census, more than three quarters of the population of foreign birth and parentage resided in urban centers. In the forty-five cities with more than 100,000 residents, which together housed more than one half of the total urban population, immigrants and their native-born children accounted for almost 60 per cent of their combined populations.

During the century under review the least urbanized section was the South, with little more than a quarter of its population so classed in 1920, but the Western states were already as urbanized as the nation as a whole, and in the Northeast more than three fourths of the people lived in cities. As might be expected, the nationwide distribution of immigrants was reflected in these regional variations, for in 1920 slightly more than 70 per cent of the entire forign-born population resided in New England and in the Middle Atlantic and North Central states. The large cities of these areas were the leading destinations of immigrants and provide the best examples of the changes in internal spatial structure of immigrant employment and residence discussed in this review.

The emphasis of this study has been on changes in the locational characteristics of the residence and employment of immigrant groups both nationally, as between cities, and locally within the physical limits of the city. A knowledge of the aggregate spatial results of urbanization yields only limited insights into the process of population concentration itself or into the ways individual migrants selected a particular destination from a range of alternatives. Clearly, the behavioral motivations of immigrants constitute an important but neglected aspect both of the cityward movement and of residential choice during the nineteenth century. Yet it is also apparent that similar patterns of antecedent behavior did not necessarily result in identical locational choices. Although stochastic and occasionally cybernetic models have been used increasingly to describe behavioral processes in the concentration and relocation of individuals in space, changes in the extent and complexity of the location and internal spatial arrangement of urban centers are defined by the technological and organizational capacities of particular groups at a particular time.[1]

The steady increase in urbanization during the nineteenth century reflects a cumulative adaptation to the opportunities of the growing resource base and accelerating technological advance. Rapid growth was in part a spatial adjustment to shifts in the occupational distribution. Most migrants sought new occupations as well as new residential locations; consequently, the changing distribution of new sources of employment between regions and within cities limited the range of possible destinations. The changes in the destinations of successive flows of immigrants thus was related to the effects of the progressive enlargement and differentiation of the national economy upon the pattern of new employment. However, locational limitations imposed by the need for housing and employment did allow considerable latitude in the choice of destination from among a small group of suitable cities or within a particular city. Under these circumstances, we must assume that previous contacts, the availability of information on potential destinations, personal perception, cultural preference, and a variety of fortuitous incidents influenced the final choice.

That there was much freedom of individual choice within the constraints imposed by need to settle in locations with available and appropriate employment opportunities is clear from the mobility of individual immigrants between neighborhoods of the same city and between different urban centers. The rapidity of such population turnover has only recently been documented, and only for a limited number of urban areas, but it would appear from these pioneer investigations that only about one third of the total number of households in any one urban neighborhood remained there for as long as a decade.[2] Certainly part of the turnover resulted from death, relocation, or commercial and industrial expansion, but many urban residents also moved from city to city. In particular, casual laborers with insecure jobs probably found it easier to move between cities than from the inner core to the periphery of the same city. Most urban residents who could afford the increased costs lived in the inner suburbs—today considered integral parts of the central city.

At present we do not have adequate evidence of immigrants' destinations and the amount of turnover in cities after 1880, when the source areas of foreign immigrants shifted to southern and eastern Europe and when Negroes from the South added substantially to internal migration. Nor can we state with assurance whether high rates of population turnover radically altered the physical and social characteristics in residential districts, for an exchange of residents did not always change the aggregate characteristics of an area. Whatever its other effects, population mobility did not obliterate or badly obscure the cumulative locational effects of the selective migration of people from different source areas.

The volume, time of arrival, and destinations of urban immigrants reflected changes in the spatial extent and complexity of the national economy, with the result that the proportions of immigrants in cities varied throughout the country. In spite of population movements, both national and within cities since about 1920, and in spite of the assimilation of most foreign groups after two or three generations, racial, religious, and to a decreasing degree ethnic or national identities were maintained until quite recently by limited intermarriage between groups.[3] Conspicuous regional variations in the proportions of people of different religions indicate in part the residual effects of the selective migration of different groups.[4] Moreover, racial and religious differences and prejudices within cities continue to complicate residential choices based primarily upon socio-economic status, although it is possible that, because of increased personal mobility, propinquity is no longer essential to maintaining social, religious, or ethnic ties.[5] The increased pace of urbanization and the internal spatial differentiation of cities during the nineteenth and early twentieth centuries bequeathed not only many physical problems to the modern planner, but also the racial and religious pluralism of most American cities.

NOTES

1. E. E. Lampard, "The Evolving System of Cities in the United States: Urbanization and Economic Development," in H. S. Perloff and L. Wingo, Jr., eds., *Issues in Urban Economics,* Baltimore, 1968, pp. 81-138.
2. S. Thernstrom, *Poverty and Progress: Social Mobility in the Nineteenth Century City,* Cambridge, 1964, pp. 192-224; P. R. Knights, "Population Turnover, Persistence and Residential Mobility in Boston, 1830-60," in S. Thernstrom and R. Sennett, eds., *Nineteenth Century Cities, Essays in the New Urban History,* New Haven, 1969, pp. 258-74.
3. M. M. Gordon, *Assimilation in American Life,* New York, 1968, pp. 160-232; W. Herberg, *Protestant, Catholic, Jew, An Essay in Religious Sociology,* Garden City, N.Y., 1960, pp. 1-45.
4. W. Zelinsky, "An Approach to the Religious Geography of the United States: Patterns of Church Membership in 1952," *Annals of the Association of American Geographers,* 51, 1961, pp. 139-93.
5. M. M. Webber, "The Urban Place and the Nonplace Urban Realm," in M. M. Webber et. al., *Explorations into Urban Structure,* Philadelphia, 1964, pp. 108-14.

BIBLIOGRAPHY

Abbott, E. *The Tenements of Chicago: 1908-1935*, Chicago, 1936.

Adams, W. F. *Ireland and the Irish Immigration to the New World from 1815 to the Famine*, New Haven, 1932.

Albion, R. G. "New York Port and Its Disappointed Rivals, 1815-1860," *Journal of Economic and Business History*, 3, 1930-31, pp. 602-29.

————. *The Rise of New York Port, 1815-1860*, Hamden, 1939.

Alonso, W. "The Historic and the Structural Theories of Urban Form: Their Limitations and Urban Renewal," *Land Economics*, 40, 1964, pp. 227-31.

————. *Location and Land Use*, Cambridge, 1964.

Anderson, T. R. "Social and Economic Factors Affecting the Location of Residential Neighborhoods," *Papers and Proceedings of the Regional Science Asociation*, 9, 1962, pp. 161-70.

Aronovici, C. "The Cost of a Decent Home," *Forum*, 58, 1914, pp. 111-12.

Aydelotte, W. O. "Quantification in History," *American Historical Review*, 71, 1966, pp. 803-82.

Baldwin, R. "Patterns of Development in Newly Settled Regions," *Manchester School of Economic and Social Studies*, 24, 1956, pp. 161-79.

Belcher, W. W. *The Economic Rivalry Between St. Louis and Chicago, 1850-1880*, New York, 1947.

Bernheimer, C. S., ed. *The Rusian Jew in the United States*, Philadelphia, 1905.

Berry, B. J. L. "City Size Distribution and Economic Development," *Economic Development and Cultural Change*, 9, 1961, pp. 573-88.

————. *Geography of Market Centers and Retail Distribution*, Englewood Cliffs, N.J., 1967.

Bidwell, P. W. "Population Growth in Southern New England, 1810-1860," *Publications of the American Statistical Association*, New Series, 15, 1916-17, pp. 813-39.

Billings, J. S. "Municipal Sanitation: Defects in American Cities," *Forum*, 15, 1893, 304-10.

Borchert, J. R. "American Metropolitan Evolution," *Geographical Review,* 57, 1967, pp. 301-32.

Bridenbaugh, C. *Cities in Revolt, Urban Life in America, 1743-1776,* New York, 1955.

Brindisi, R. "The Italian and Public Health," *Charities,* 12, 1904, pp. 443-504.

Brush, J. E. and Gauthier, H. L., Jr. "Service Centers and Consumer Trips: Studies on the Philadelphia Metropolitan Fringe," *Department of Geography Research Paper No. 113,* Chicago, 1968.

Burgess, E. W. "The Growth of the City," in Park, R. E., ed., *The City,* Chicago, 1922, pp. 47-62.

Burghardt, A. F. "The Location of River Towns in the Central Lowlands of the United States," *Annals of the Association of American Geographers,* 69, 1959, pp. 305-23.

Careless, J. M. S. "Frontierism, Metropolitanism and Canadian History," *Canadian Historical Review,* 37, 1950, pp. 1-21.

Cargill, H. L. "Small Houses for Workingmen," in De Forest R. W. and Veiller, L., eds., *The Tenement House Problem,* Vol. 1, New York, 1903, pp. 331-32.

Carpenter, N. "Immigrants and Their Children," *U.S. Bureau of the Census Monograph,* No. 7, Washington, D.C., 1927.

Christaller, W. *The Central Places of Southern Germany,* trans., C. Baskin, Englewood Cliffs, N.J., 1966.

Claghorn, Kate H. "Foreign Immigrants in New York City," *Report of the Industrial Commission,* 14, 1901, pp. 449-91.

Clark, G. E. "Sanitary Improvement in New York During the Last Quarter of a Century," *Popular Science Monthly,* 39, 1891, pp. 319-30.

Clark, J. G. *The Grain Trade of the Old Northwest,* Urbana, 1966.

Curti, M. L. *The Making of an American Community,* Stanford, 1959.

Dublin, L. I. "The Mortality of Foreign Race Stocks in Pennsylvania and New York, 1910," *Quarterly Publication of the American Statistical Association,* 17, 1920-21, pp. 13-44.

Elsing, W. T. "Life in New York Tenement Houses as Seen by a City Missionary," in Woods, R. A., ed., *The Poor in Great Cities,* New York, 1895, pp. 42-85.

Ernst, R. *Immigrant Life in New York City: 1825-1863,* New York, 1949.

Farnie, D. A. "The Commercial Empire of the Atlantic, 1607-1783," *Economic History Review,* 2nd Series, 15, 1962, pp. 205-18.

Faust, A. B. *The German Element in the United States,* Boston and New York, 1909.

Fellman, J. D. "Pre-Building Growth Patterns in Chicago," *Annals of the Association of American Geographers,* 47, 1957, pp. 59-82.

Firey, W. I. *Land Use in Central Boston,* Cambridge, 1948.

———. "Sentiment and Symbolism as Ecological Variables," *American Sociological Review,* 10, 1945, pp. 140-48.

Fishberg, M. "Health and Sanitation of the Immigrant Jewish Population of New York," *The Menorah,* 33, 1902, pp. 37-46, 73-82, 168-80.

Fishlow, A. *Railroads and the Transformation of the Ante-Bellum Economy,* Cambridge, 1967.

Fletcher, H. J. "The Doom of the Small Town," *Forum,* 19, 1895, p. 214-23.

Foerster, R. F. *The Italian Emigration of Our Times,* Cambridge, 1919.

Fogel, R. W. "A Quantitative Approach to the Study of Railroads in American Economic Growth," *Journal of Economic History,* 22, 1962, pp. 163-97.

————. "American Interregional Trade in the Nineteenth Century," in Andreano, R. L., ed., *New Views of American Economic Development,* Cambridge, 1965, pp. 213-24.

Ford, J. *Slums and Housing,* Cambridge, 1936.

Frazier, E. F. "Negro Harlem: An Ecological Study," *American Journal of Sociology,* 1937, pp. 72-88.

Friedmann, J. "Regional Economic Policy for Developing Areas," *Papers and Proceedings of the Regional Science Association,* 11, 1963, pp. 41-61.

Gans, H. J. *The Urban Villagers,* New York, 1962.

Gates, C. M. "The Role of Cities in the Westward Movement," *Mississippi Valley Historical Review,* 37, 1950, pp. 277-78.

Gates, Paul W. *The Illinois Central Railroad and Its Colonization Work,* Cambridge, 1936.

Geddes, P. E. *Cities in Evolution,* London, rev. ed., 1949.

Glazer, N. and Moynihan, D. P. *Beyond the Melting Pot,* Cambridge, 1963.

Goheen, Peter G. "Victorian Toronto, 1850-1900: Pattern and Process of Growth," *Department of Geography Research Paper No. 127,* Chicago, 1970.

Gordon, M. M. *Assimilation in American Life,* New York, 1968.

Gould, C. P. "The Economic Causes of the Rise of Baltimore," in *Essays in Colonial History Presented to Charles McLean Andrews,* New Haven, 1931, pp. 235-38.

Gras, N. S. B. *An Introduction to Economic History,* New York, 1922.

Guilfoy, W. H. "The Death Rate of the City of New York as Affected by the Cosmopolitan Character of Its Population," *Quarterly Publications of the American Statistical Association,* 10, 1907, pp. 515-22.

Guillet, E. C. *The Great Migration: The Atlantic Crossing by Sailing Ship Since 1770,* Toronto, 1963.

Gustagson, W. E. "Printing and Publishing" in Hall, M., ed., *Made in New York,* Cambridge, 1959, pp. 137-54.

Hagerstrand, T. "Migration and Area, Survey of a Sample of Swedish Migration Fields and Hypothetical Considerations of Their Genesis," *Lund Studies in Geography,* Series B, 13, 1957, pp. 27-154.

Haig, R. M. "Towards an Understanding of the Metropolis," *Quarterly Journal of Economics,* 40, 1926, pp. 179-208.

Handlin, O. *Boston's Immigrants: A Study in Acculturation,* Cambridge, 1959.

Hansen, M. L. *The Mingling of the Canadian and American Peoples,* New Haven, 1940.

———. "The Second Colonization of New England," *New England Quarterly,* 2, 1929, pp. 539-60.

Hawgood, J. A. *The Tragedy of German-America,* New York, 1940.

Hays, S. P. "The Use of Archives for Historical Statistical Inquiry," *Journal of the National Archives,* 1, 1969, pp. 7-15.

Hazard, B. E. *The Organization of the Boot and Shoe Industry in Massachusetts Before 1875,* Cambridge, 1921.

Helfgott, R. B. "Women's and Children's Apparel," in Hall, M., ed., *Made in New York,* Cambridge, 1959, pp. 47-52.

Herberg, W. *Protestant, Catholic, Jew: An Essay in Religious Sociology,* Garden City, N.Y., 1960.

Higgs, R. "The Growth of Cities in a Midwestern Region, 1870-1900," *Journal of Regional Science,* 9, 1969, pp. 369-75.

Hilliard, S. B. "Pork in the Ante-Bellum South: The Geography of Self-Sufficiency," *Annals of the Association of American Geographers,* 59, 1969, pp. 461-80.

Hoffman, F. L. "American Mortality Progress During the Last Half Century," in Ravenal, Mazyck P., ed., *A Half Century of Public Health,* New York, 1921, pp. 94-117.

———. "The General Death Rate of Large American Cities: 1871-1904," *Quarterly Publications of the American Statistical Association,* 10, 1906-7, pp. 1-75.

Homans, G. C. *The Human Group,* New York, 1950.

Hoover, E. M. "The Location of the Shoe Industry in the United States," *Quarterly Journal of Economics,* 47, 1933, pp. 254-76.

Hoover, E. M. and Vernon, R. *Anatomy of a Metropolis,* Cambridge, 1959.

Hourwich, I. A. *Immigration and Labor: The Economic Aspects of European Immigration to the United States,* New York, 1912.

Hower, R. M. *History of Macy's of New York, 1858-1919,* Cambridge, 1943.

Hoyt, H. *The Structure and the Growth of Residential Neighborhoods in American Cities,* Washington, D.C., 1939.

Hozelitz, B. F. "The City, the Factory and Economic Growth," *American Economic Review,* 45, 1955, pp. 166-84.

Hunter, L. C. *Steamboats on Western Rivers, American Economic and Technical History,* Cambridge, 1949.

Hurd, R. M. *Principles of City Land Values,* New York, 1903.

Isard, W. "A Neglected Cycle: The Transport Building Cycle," *Revue of Economic Statistics,* 24, 1942, pp. 149-58.

———. "Transport Developments and Building Cycles," *Quarterly Journal of Economics,* 57, 1942, pp. 90-112.

Janson, F. E. *The Background of Swedish Immigration, 1840-1930,* Philadelphia, 1931.

Jones, M. A. *American Immigration,* Chicago, 1962.

Joseph, S. *Jewish Immigration to the United States from 1881 to 1910,* New York, 1914.

Kennedy, C. G. "Commuter Services in the Boston Area 1835 to 1860," *Business History Review,* 26, 1962, pp. 277-87.

Kirkland, E. C. *Industry Comes of Age,* New York, 1961.

―――. *Men, Cities and Transportation: A Study in New England History, 1820-1900,* Volume 1, Cambridge, 1948.

Knights, Peter R. "Population Turnover, Persistence and Residential Mobility in Boston, 1830-60," in Thernstrom, S. and Sennett, R., eds., *Nineteenth Century Cities, Essays in the New Urban History,* New Haven, 1969, pp. 258-74.

Kuznets, S. "Introduction: Population Redistribution, Migration, and Economic Growth," in Eldridge, H. T. and Thomas, D. S., *Population Redistribution and Economic Growth, United States, 1870-1950,* Volume 3, *Demographic Analyses and Interrelations,* Philadelphia, 1964, pp. xxiii-xxxv.

Lampard, E. E. "American Historians and the Study of Urbanization," *American Historical Review,* 67, 1961, pp. 49-61.

―――. "Historical Aspects of Urbanization," in Hauser, P. M. and Schnore, L. F., eds., *The Study of Urbanization,* New York, 1965, pp. 519-54.

―――. "The Evolving System of Cities in the United States: Urbanization and Economic Development," in Perloff, H. S. and Wingo, L., Jr., eds., *Issues in Urban Economics,* Baltimore, 1968, pp. 81-138.

―――. "The History of Cities in the Economically Advanced Areas," *Economic Development and Cultural Change,* 3, 1955, pp. 81-136.

Lemon, J. T. "Urbanization and the Development of Eighteenth Century Southeastern Pennsylvania and Adjacent Delaware," *William and Mary Quarterly,* 3d Series, 24, 1967, pp. 501-42.

Library of Congress. *Immigration in the United States: A Selected List of References,* Washington, 1943.

Livingood, J. W. *The Philadelphia-Baltimore Trade Rivalry, 1780-1860,* Harrisburg, 1947.

Lord, E., et al. *The Italian in America,* New York, 1905.

Lowi, T. J. *At the Pleasure of the Mayor: Power and Patronage in New York City: 1898-1958,* New York, 1964.

Lubove, R. *The Progressives and the Slums,* Pittsburgh, 1962.

Lukermann, F. "Empirical Expressions of Nodality and Hierarchy in a Circulation Manifold," *East Lakes Geographer,* 2, 1966, pp. 17-44.

Madden, C. H. "On Some Indicators of Stability in the Growth of Cities in the United States," *Economic Development and Cultural Change,* 4, 1955-56, pp. 236-52.

Marburg, T. "Domestic Trade and Marketing," in Williamson, H. F., ed., *The Growth of the American Economy,* New York, 1951, pp. 511-31.

Mason, E. S. *The Street Railway in Massachusetts,* Cambridge, 1932.

Massachusetts House Document, No. 475, 1898, *Report of the Special Commission on the Relation Between Cities and Street Railroad Companies,* Boston, 1898.

Mayer, H. M. *The Railway Pattern of Metropolitan Chicago,* Chicago, 1943.

McKelvey, B. *The Urbanization of America, 1865-1915,* New Brunswick, 1963.

McManis, D. R. "The Initial Evaluation and Utilization of the Illinois Prairies, 1815-1840," *Department of Geography Research Paper No. 94,* Chicago, 1964.

Merrens, H. R. *Colonial North Carolina in the Eighteenth Century: A Study in Historical Geography,* Chapel Hill, 1964.

Middleton, A. P. *Tobacco Coast, A Maritime History of Chesapeake Bay in the Colonial Era,* ed. George C. Mason, Newport News, 1953, p. 353.

Mood, F. "Studies in the History of American Settled Areas and Frontier Lines, 1625-1790," *Agricultural History,* 26, 1952, pp. 16-34.

Moore, W. E. *The Impact of Industry,* Englewood Cliffs, N.J., 1965.

Morison, S. E., *The Maritime History of Massachusetts, 1783-1860,* Cambridge, 1921.

Morrill, R. L. "Migration and the Spread and Growth of Urban Settlement," *Lund Studies in Geography,* Series B, 26, 1965.

Moses, L. S. and Williamson, H. F., Jr., "The Location of Economic Activity in Cities," *American Economic Review,* 57, 1967, pp. 211-22.

Murdie, R. A. "The Factorial Ecology of Metropolitan Toronto, 1951-1961: An Essay on the Social Geography of the City," *Department of Geography Research Paper No. 116,* Chicago, 1968.

North, D. C. *The Economic Growth of the United States, 1790-1860,* Englewood Cliffs, N.J., 1961.

Nourse, Edwin G. *The Chicago Produce Market,* Boston and New York, 1918.

Nystrom, P. H. *Economics of Retailing,* Volume 1, New York, 1915.

Osofsky, G. *The Making of a Ghetto,* New York, 1967.

Overton, R. C. *Burlington West: A Colonization History of the Burlington West,* Cambridge, 1941.

Page, T. W. "The Transportation of Immigrants and Reception Arrangements in the Nineteenth Century," *Journal of Political Economy,* 19, 1911, pp. 732-49.

Park, R. E. and Miller, H. A. *Old World Traits Transplanted,* New York, 1921.

Perloff, H. S., et. al. *Regions, Resources and Economic Growth,* Baltimore, 1960.

Perloff, H. S. and Wingo, L., Jr. "Natural Resource Endowment and Regional Economic Growth," in Spengler, J. J., ed., *Natural Resources and Economic Growth,* Washington, D.C., 1961, pp. 191-212.

Pope, J. *The Clothing Industry in New York,* Columbia, Mo., 1905.

Pratt, E. E. *Industrial Causes of Congestion of Population in New York City,* New York, 1911.

Pred, A. R. "Industrialization, Initial Advantage and American Metropolitan Growth," *Geographical Review*, 55, 1965, pp. 158-85.

————. "Manufacturing in the American Mercantile City: 1800-1840," *Annals of the Association of American Geographers*, 56, 1966, pp. 307-38.

————. "The External Relations of Cities During the Industrial Revolution," *Department of Geography Research Paper No. 76*, Chicago, 1962.

————. "The Intrametropolitan Location of American Manufacturing," *Annals of the Association of American Geographers*, 54, 1964, pp. 165-80.

————. *The Spatial Dynamics of U.S. Urban-Industrial Growth, 1800-1914: Interpretative and Theoretical Essays*, Cambridge, 1966.

Quiett, G. C. *They Built the West: An Epic of Rails and Cities*, New York, 1934.

Rannells, J. *The Core of the City*, New York, 1956.

Ransom, R. L. "Canals and Development: A Discussion of Issues," *Papers and Proceedings of the American Economic Association*, 54, 1964, pp. 365-76.

————. "Interregional Canals and Economic Specialization in the Ante-Bellum United States," *Explorations in Entrepreneurial History*, 5, 1967, pp. 12-35.

Ravenstein, E. G. "The Laws of Migration," *Journal of the Royal Statistical Society*, 52, 1889, pp. 241-301.

Riggleman, J. R. "Building Cycles in the United States, 1875-1932," *Journal of the American Statistical Association*, 28, 1933, pp. 174-83.

Roberts, P. *The New Immigration: A Study of the Industrial and Social Life of Southeast Europeans in America*, New York, 1913.

Rodwin, L. *Housing and Economic Progress: A Study of the Housing Experiences of Boston's Middle-Income Families*, Cambridge, 1961.

Rothstein, M. "Ante-Bellum Wheat and Cotton Exports: A Contrast in Marketing Organization and Economic Development," *Agricultural History*, 40, 1966, pp. 91-100.

————. "The Ante-Bellum South as a Dual Economy: A Tentative Hypothesis," *Agricultural History*, 41, 1967, pp. 373-82.

Rubin, J. "Urban Growth and Development," in Gilchrist, D. T., ed., *The Growth of Seaport Cities: 1790-1825*, Charlottesville, 1967, pp. 3-21.

Sanborn, A. F. "The Anatomy of a Tenement Street," *Forum*, 18, 1894, pp. 554-72.

Scheiber, H. N. "Urban Rivalry and Internal Improvement in the Old North West," *Ohio History*, 71-72, 1962-63, pp. 227-39.

Schnore, L. F. "On the Spatial Structure of Cities in the Two Americas," in Hauser, P. F. and Schnore, L. F., eds., *The Study of Urbanization*, New York, 1965, pp. 347-98.

Sjoberg, G. *The Pre-industrial City*, New York, 1960.

Smelser, N. J. *Social Change in the Industrial Revolution—An Application of Theory to the British Cotton Industry: 1770-1840*, Chicago, 1959.

Smerk, G. M. "The Streetcar: Shape of American Cities," *Traffic Quarterly*, 21, 1967, pp. 569-84.

Smolensky, E. and Ratejczak, D. "The Conception of Cities," *Explorations in Entrepreneurial History*, 2nd Series, 2, 1965, pp. 90-131.

Spear, A. H. *Black Chicago: The Making of a Negro Ghetto, 1890-1920*, Chicago, 1967.

Still, B. "Patterns of Mid-Nineteenth Century Urbanization in the Middle West," *Mississippi Valley Historical Review*, 28, 1941, pp. 187-206.

Stilwell, L. D. "Migration from Vermont: 1776-1860," *Proceedings of the Vermont Historical Society*, 5, 1937, pp. 63-246.

Stouffer, A. "Intervening Opportunities: A Theory Relating to Mobility and Distance," *American Sociological Review*, 5, 1940, pp. 845-67.

Streightoff, F. H. *Standard of Living Among the Industrial People of America*, Boston and New York, 1911.

Taylor, G. R. *Satellite Cities: A Study of Industrial Suburbs*, New York, 1915.

Taylor, G. R. "American Economic Growth Before 1840: An Exploratory Essay," *Journal of Economic History*, 24, 1964, pp. 427-44.

————. "American Urban Growth Preceding the Railway Age," *Journal of Economic History*, 27, 1967, pp. 309-39.

————. *The Transportation Revolution*, New York, 1951.

Thernstrom, S. *Poverty and Progress: Social Mobility in a Nineteenth Century City*, Cambridge, 1964.

Thernstrom, S. and Sennett, R., eds. *Nineteenth-Century Cities: Essays in the New Urban History*, New Haven, 1969.

Thomas, B. *Migration and Economic Growth: A Study of Great Britain and the Atlantic Economy*, Cambridge, 1954.

Thomas, W. I. and Znaniecki, F. *Polish Peasant in Europe and America*, New York, 1927.

Thompson, W. R. *A Preface to Urban Economics*, Baltimore, 1965.

Thornthwaite, C. W. *Internal Migration in the United States*, Philadelphia, 1934.

Tunnard, C. and Reed, H. H. *American Skyline*, Boston, 1955.

Turner, F. J. "The Significance of the Frontier in American History," *Proceedings of the State Historical Society of Wisconsin*, 41, 1894, pp. 79-112.

Turner, R. E. "The Industrial City: Center of Culture Change," in Ware, C. F., ed., *The Cultural Approach to History*, New York, 1940, pp. 228-42.

Turvey, R. *The Economics of Real Property: An Analysis of Property Values and Patterns of Use*, London, 1957.

United States Federal Trade Commission, *Report on the Wholesale Marketing of Food*, Washington, D.C., 1920.

United States House Document, No. 183, 57th Congress, 1st Session, Serial No. 4344, *Report of the Industrial Commission Volumes 14 and 15*, Washington, D.C., 1907.

United States Senate Document, No. 22, 62nd Congress, 1st Session, Serial No. 6082, *Cost of Living in American Towns*, Washington, D.C., 1911.

United States Senate Document, No. 338, 61st Congress, 2nd Session, Serial No. 5665, *Report of the Immigration (Dillingham) Commission,* Washington, D.C., 1911.

United States Senate Document, No. 2309, 32nd Congress, 2nd Session, Serial No. 3140, *Report of the Committee on Manufactures on the Sweating System,* Washington, D.C., 1893.

Vance, J. E., Jr. "Emerging Patterns of Commercial Structure in American Cities," in Norborg, K., ed., *Proceedings of the IGU Symposium in Urban Geography,* Lund, 1962, pp. 484-518.

―――――. *Geography and Urban Evolution in the San Francisco Bay Area,* Berkeley, 1964.

―――――. "Labor-shed, Employment Field, and Dynamic Analysis in Urban Geography," *Economic Geography,* 36, 1960, pp. 189-220.

Vance, R. B. and Smith, S. "Metropolitan Dominance and Integration," in Vance, R. B. and Demerath, N. J., eds., *The Urban South,* Chapel Hill, 1954, pp. 114-34.

Veiller, L. "Housing Conditions and Tenement Laws in Leading American Cities," in De Forest, R. W. and Veiller, L., eds., *The Tenement House Problem,* Volume 1, New York, 1903, pp. 129-72.

Vreeland, H. H. "The Street Railways of America," in Depew, C. M., ed., *One Hundred Years of American Commerce,* New York, 1895, pp. 141-48.

Wade, R. C. *The Urban Frontier,* Cambridge, 1959.

Ward, D. "A Comparative Historical Geography of Streetcar Suburbs in Boston, Massachusetts and Leeds, England: 1850-1920," *Annals of the Association of American Geographers,* 54, 1964, pp. 447-89.

―――――. "The Emergence of Central Immigrant Ghettoes in American Cities: 1840-1920," *Annals of the Association of American Geographers,* 58, 1968, pp. 343-59.

―――――. "The Industrial Revolution and the Emergence of Boston's Central Business District," *Economy Geography,* 42, 1966, pp. 152-71.

―――――. "The Internal Spatial Structure of Immigrant Residential Districts in the Late Nineteenth Century," *Geographical Analysis,* 1, 1969, pp. 337-53.

Ware, C. F. *Greenwich Village, 1920-1930,* Boston, 1935.

Warne, F. J. *The Tide of Immigration,* New York, 1916.

Warner, S. B. Jr. *Streetcar Suburbs: The Process of Growth in Boston,* Cambridge, 1962.

―――――. *The Private City,* Philadelphia, 1967.

Webber, M. M. "The Urban Place and the Nonplace Urban Realm," in Webber, M. M., et. al., *Explorations into Urban Structure,* Philadelphia, 1964.

Weber, A. F. *The Growth of Cities in the Nineteenth Century,* New York, 1899.

Whyte, W. F. *The Street Corner Society,* Chicago, 1943.

Wilcox, W. F. "Decrease of Interstate Migration," *Political Science Quarterly,* 10, 1895, pp. 604-5.

Wilkinson, T. O. "Urban Structure and Industrialization," *American Sociological Review,* 25, 1960, pp. 353-63.

Williamson, J. G. "Antebellum Urbanization in the American Northeast," *Journal of Economic History,* 25, 1965, pp. 592-608.

Williamson, J. G. and Swanson, J. A. "The Growth of Cities in the American North East, 1820-1920," *Explorations in Entrepreneurial History,* 2nd Series, 4, 1966, supplement.

Wingate, C. F. "The City's Health—Sanitary Construction," *Municipal Affairs,* 2, 1898, pp. 261-70.

Wolfe, A. B. *The Lodging House Problem in Boston,* Cambridge, 1913.

Wood, E. E. *The Housing of the Unskilled Wage Earner,* New York, 1919.

Woods, R. A., ed. *The City Wilderness,* Boston, 1898.

Woods, R. A. and Kennedy, A. J., eds. *The Zone of Emergence,* Cambridge, 1962.

Woofter, T. J., Jr. *Negro Problems in Cities,* New York, 1928.

Zelinsky, W. "An Approach to the Religious Geography of the United States: Patterns of Church Membership in 1952," *Annals of the Association of American Geographers,* 51, 1961, pp. 139-93.

Zorbaugh, H. W. *The Gold Coast and the Slum,* Chicago, 1929.

INDEX

AA-122   bln 2